Social Media Marketing 2020

The Ultimate Step-by-Step Guide to Achieve Success, Learn the Best Beginners' Strategies to Generate Powerful Content and Influence Fans and Followers

Author Name: Harvey Quick

Description

You Are a Few Steps Away From Thriving and Making Abundant Success With All Your Social Media Marketing Campaigns!

Do you know that for you to develop a brand strategy plan, you must first create and refine the process behind your brand development strategy to grow your brand digitally? Do you want to give your brand opportunities, freedom, choice, security, and possibilities to grow and become a strong brand with a powerful social media presence and raving fans and followers?

This step-by-step, easy-to-use book shows you some of the elements of digital marketing campaigns, what makes a digital brand strategy, the keys to branding for business, and how to build effective strategies for your brand.

If you are bored with spinning the wheel when it comes to your social media marketing strategy and brand building strategy, buy this book. Its approach draws from some guidelines, tips, tactics, strategies, examples, and ways to identify significant marketing trends for 2020. How you can be good at digital marketing in 2020 is not something easy to come by, particularly with the advancements and changing trends in digital technologies. You need to know how to create a social media marketing plan for

2020 and understand how you will win at social media marketing in 2020 and beyond is quite necessary for your brand.

In this book, what you will find include:

- How you can dig into what your competitors are doing on social media and how you can beat them in the game

- How you can establish the essential metrics in your social media content strategy

- Viable ways to reach, acquire and engage your target audience

- How you can increase your brand awareness on social media

- How your brand can obtain a higher quality of sales

- How you can address your biggest challenges with set goals

- How you can keep your followers happy by providing exceptional customer service

- What to do to generate conversation around your brand on social media channels

- What is brand recognition and what is the process of accomplishing it

- The perfect yet simple ways to optimize your social media profiles

- How to choose the right social media networks for your brand

- The powerful yet simple ways to interact with your followers to increase engagement

- What you need to do and the way to go about understanding your audience and figure out their needs

- The best practices to use hashtags on some social media channels (it's entirely not what you think)

- What are the effective ways to put a personal touch to your interactions with your customers on social media

- What are the best ways to handle complaints and negative feedback (with detailed tips and strategies, so your brand doesn't lose customers)

- Why voice and tone matter to your social media

- What are the social media content that will give your brand the most exceptional value

- Social media marketing mistakes you need to avoid

- Useful tips for social media marketing on social media channels to increase growth and sales

Plus, plenty of examples, scientific study findings, and rules of improving negative feedback and managing social media crisis.

If you'd like some tips about establishing your audience and know exactly what they want, buy this book.

If you'd like to know the kind of social media content to develop and post to convert people into followers and then into raving fans, buy this book.

This book will change the way you look at social media marketing. It will change your life forever.

Click the "Buy Now" button at the top of this page and get your copy.

Table of Contents

Introduction

Congratulations on purchasing *Social Media Marketing 2020: The Ultimate Step-By-Step Guide to Achieve Success, Learn the Best Beginner's Strategy to Generate Powerful Content and Influence Fans and Followers*, and thank you for doing so.

Every day, almost all brands come online to implement social media marketing, and downloading this book is an excellent step for you to having a clear understanding of the world of social media marketing. Usually, everything about social media marketing can be quite tricky since there are different social media channels, and each with individual personalized strategies to use them for prospect targeting and engagement. In this book, you will see examples of all of these social media marketing plans and strategies, how to set up your account on each platform to have full visibility, and also how to interact and engage your audience.

To this end, some of the chapters in this book will discuss social media development, what social media marketing is, and how to create a social media marketing plan for 2020. The book shows some practical examples of how digital marketing works, how to choose the right social media, and how you can optimize your social media profiles for maximum engagement. And this is where some of the chapters in this book become quite useful as you will learn about building social media following and developing a content calendar so you can keep your followers actively engaged.

With a clear perception of some of these factors out of the way, this book will discuss some ways you and your brand can use to improve your brand awareness, improve brand loyalty, and increase traffic, all with robust yet straightforward examples. Then, the book will go more in-depth on finding and using the right tone and voice for your social media marketing.

On the shelves, there are plenty of books on social media marketing, and we will like to thank you for making this one your choice! We are making all efforts to be sure that this book has all the practical and necessary information to help you in your marketing efforts. Thank you once again!

Chapter 1: What Is Social Media Marketing?

Over the past decades, there have been drastic changes in buying behaviors. And to show how effective digital marketing works, consumers are beginning, and most times, ending their buyers' journey online. Regardless of industry or size, for any business that attempts to compete in the modern marketplace, digital marketing is a necessity based on the way consumers buy products and services, as well as the shift in the way that they make purchase decisions.

For any business to engage as they reach their audience using the right campaign tactics strategically, have a clear understanding of how digital marketing works is quite essential. With this book, any business will have an easy walkthrough on specific elements in delighting, converting, and attracting consumers online. And for any company to make more informed decisions about their digital marketing campaigns, this book will cover everything they need to know about how digital marketing works.

What is digital marketing?

Digital marketing is all about utilizing other digital channels to promote brands and products. Some businesses aim to reach a particular audience and to help them achieve these target consumers through the internet and other digital avenues; they need the help of digital marketing. For several companies and marketers to get their target audience, they make use of some different digital technologies. Also, for them to engage and attract their target consumers, they use social media, mobile technology such as smartphones, email marketing, PPC and display ads, and other mediums in addition to their website.

Because of the way consumers make purchasing decisions is as a result of the significant role of the internet, digital marketing is crucial for modern business. Also, how consumers purchase their products and services has an excellent impact on the internet. As a result, not only do companies need to amplify their visibility as much as possible, but they also must be present online. Gone are the days of requesting more information about products as consumers browse at a physical store location. Now, though they make a decision to visit the physical store for their final purchase, to get the required information for making an informed purchase, consumers use the internet. Here, digital marketing becomes vital since wherever consumers can be in their journey as digital buyers, digital marketing helps a business reach them.

How digital marketing works

So that businesses can execute smarter decisions about their digital marketing campaigns, it is quite critical for business owners to have a clear understanding of how digital marketing works. When they have learned to recognize how each element can aid their marketing goals after they know each of these elements, then, they will have all they need to understand digital marketing. Below are the explanations of how businesses can use each one of these digital marketing tactics for their business.

Website marketing:

The cornerstone of any business' digital marketing strategy, in many ways, is their company's website. As the site is the place where your leads will finally convert into paying customers, more often than not, your website is the hub where some of your target customers get your brand's initial impression. As to how digital marketing works, it is imperative to discuss how your website plays a role.

For you to attract, engage, and convert leads is the goal of digital marketing. You will have the power to lead your target customers back to your website to make a purchase or get more information when you implement some of these tactics. In your target market, to make an excellent first impression with consumers, sometimes, your website is your brand's only chance. As a result, the graphics and colors you use to design your site, as well as the entire layout, are some of the things you must pay close attention to. When people find the layout and content to be unattractive, 38 percent of people will stop engaging with a website, according to Adobe.

However, the crucial thing is not only the appearance of your site. Other significant aspects are the design and optimization for conversion because your website is the center of several of your digital marketing campaigns. You must create a site that is quite easy to read and navigate and to move further down the funnel, with clear guidance for the next steps consumers need to take. You must also not leave the mobile users behind, and to enhance the mobile user's site experience, your site must be optimized for mobile devices.

Search engine optimization:

In the way digital marketing works, search engine optimization, SEO, plays a significant role. Search engines are the initial step you must take when, in this digital age, you want to reach and convert consumers. Seventy-one percent of consumers begin their buyer's journey on a search engine such as Google, according to the recent Forrester research. Then, you will be missing out on a powerful opportunity to reach and convert a significant amount of leads if you are not taking the right steps to improve your site's SEO.

So that the content of your site will be visible, accessible, and appeal to the search engines, you have to engage in the process of optimizing the content with search engine optimization. For increasing visibility in your target market, the purpose of SEO is to rank higher on the search engine results page, SERP. You will have more organic traffic, which you can drive back to your website when you have a higher rank on the SERP. Not only will the leads you are bringing into your site are of higher quality, but you will also have more traffic to your site with the use of search engine optimization. SEO is the door to attract the right person to your products and services when you are doing digital marketing. And you can reach those who are most likely to be interested in your products or services when, within your content, you have an emphasis on specific, targeted keywords.

Content marketing:

Digital marketing works along with another essential tactic, which is content marketing. When your company promotes after creating content assets aimed for the engagement and attraction of your target customers is all about content marketing. And for some different purposes, you can create these content assets, and they include retaining customers, boosting leads, increasing traffic to site, and generating brand awareness. There will always be a need for you to create content to support your leads irrespective of tactics that, as one of the aspects of your digital marketing strategy, you tend to utilize. For individuals that subscribe to your email list, this process can be as simple and short email to thank them. Or for the description and provision of information about one of the biggest challenges your target customers face, it can be a more detailed, extensive piece such as an e-book. To support your goals of a digital marketing campaign, here are some content marketing types:

- Ad content

- Podcast

- Infographics

- Images

- Videos

- Testimonials

- Case studies

- White papers

- E-books

- Posts for social media

- Blog posts

- Website pages

You will need to choose topics that appeal most to your audience strategically, and that is quite vital during the creation of valuable content assets for your digital marketing support. Ensure that you perform research on the target audience if you haven't done that already. And for you to identify the content type that can engages and attract your target customers at every point of the buyer's journey and also to ensure you know your customers quite well, you must create customer personas.

Social media marketing:

For some businesses to drive more traffic to their websites and also maintain the campaigns of their digital marketing, they utilize social media marketing. For your target customers' engagement, social media marketing involves promoting your content on social channels such as Pinterest, LinkedIn, Instagram, Twitter, and Facebook. Businesses use this tactic to improve customer engagement and increase brand awareness in their digital marketing strategy.

Businesses can reach a wider audience online, and one of the social media marketing's biggest appeals is this aspect. For example, active on Facebook are 79 percent of Americans that use the internet. You may be putting money on the table and turning your brand away from reaching new leads if, on the social media platform, your brand has no intention of engaging and reaching these potential consumers. Social media will give all of your efforts to other digital marketing the necessary support as its tactic. For example, you can drive traffic to the landing page for download when, using social media, to promote an informative eBook your brand develops, which speaks to the pain points of your target audience. And as a way to generate further interest for the content piece, and for future social media posts, you can then re-purpose parts of the eBook.

PPC advertising:

Your business must not shun the value it can get from pay-per-click, PPC ads even though bringing sufficient organic traffic is your digital marketing strategy goal. All the time a new lead clicks on your ad, the involvement of paying ad publisher is the type advertising of PPC ads. And through Google Ads, it is undoubtedly on the first page of the search engine results that your brand will appear. It may occur to you that you have been working on improving the SEO of your site, then why should you go for ads? It may take some time for SEO to begin doing its magic even though it is essential. You can see fast results through PPC ads for relevant search terms on the first page of the search engine results. Searchers are more likely to find and click on your site when your brand can gain new visibility by appearing on the first page of the SERP.

As PPC helps you ensure that you get qualified leads, these ads also generate more traffic to your site. For the relevant products and services topics, consumers will be the ones to click on your PPC ads as they search on these topics. Your services, products, or brand that you provide are more likely to interest them.

Email marketing:

Digital marketing works through another puzzling piece called email marketing. For communication with their relevant consumers, businesses use branded emails. As a means of announcing special promotions, establishing industry leadership, and increase brand awareness, marketing emails are most times used to promote events. Your campaign goals will have ultimate dependence on your marketing email content. And to support your digital marketing campaigns, develop some of this content for your email marketing:

- Based on your customers' buying behavior or browsing history, you may suggest additional content assets or products that may interest them.

- After someone has downloaded content from your site, and before recommending another relevant content piece, send them an email as a lead to thank them for their interest.

- For the delivery of company updates and the latest content from your business, craft a periodical newsletter for your subscribers.

- Concerning discounts and upcoming sales, develop promotional material straight to the inbox of the consumer.

- To let them know what they can expect to see from your brand emails, when new users subscribe to your marketing email list, send a welcome email.

Email marketing nurtures leads once they have shown interest as it is for new leads generation. Also, for your customer retention campaigns aspect, you can make use of email marketing. Indeed, for driving customer retention, one of the nest tactics is email marketing, as reported by 80 percent of retail professionals in the eMarketer study. It may be useful for you not to use email marketing alone, like the other tactics mentioned above. For leads engagement and promotion about individual sales or discounts, you might develop a monthly newsletter. However, for your other campaign tactics support, such as social media and content marketing, you can also use email marketing.

For example, for the sake of raising buzz for a new product that your brand intends to launch soon and generate new leads, you may want to hold a social media contest. For this campaign support on social media, you may turn to email marketing. More people will be aware of the competition and probably want to be part of it when you let your subscribers know about the game. Also, as a means of getting more traffic to your social media channel and even your contest, you can include links to your social media pages in each email that you send to customers and leads

.

Chapter 2: Social Media Development

Critical for the success of the web-related company is social media development. To better serve users and to improve their rankings, a social signal is what search engines now look for and to engage and educate your audience; it is essentially more than before to utilize different social media channels. Social presence is a must for your business even when your business is brick-and-mortar, only online, one location or 100, or employs one staff or 10,000. Most times, owners of business fall victim to the idea that they must be everywhere, thereby the sense of them managing their social media strategy overwhelmed them. It is no wonder so many plans fail with the consideration of several social platforms available such as Twitter, Facebook, Instagram, WhatsApp, Snapchat, Pinterest, LinkedIn, Google+, Periscope, and some others.

Proper utilization of social media and other social networking opportunities is one of the crucial components of an effective online presence. Since your business can target and leverage its audience by way of promotions, calls to actions, social referrals, and social engagement, social media sites can be quite essential.

How to choose the social networks that are right for your brand

For the determination of the active platforms of your ideal consumers, there are specific questions that you need to ask yourself.

- Will it be a translation for audience attention's new competition when you have more users on a network like Facebook?

- Is there any active presence of your customers or spending time on the web? Is it anywhere in your demographic? It is a bad idea to have your effort focus on different channels such as Snapchat if you are not targeting Millennials.

- Is there any presence for your industry?

- For your content, does the platform correlate with it? Have little focus on channels such as Periscope or YouTube if it doesn't make sense to you or you're not planning a video strategy.

- For your YouTube content creation, do you have the tools, budget, and time? Does it even make sense to you as the owner of the business?

You can develop a persona for buyers/customers if you don't have any clue of the types of people your customers are, and you can know their expectation from you, how they act, and who they are? And from the content of your social media to your website content and even more, this persona can be a guide for everything. Irrespective of demographic, niche, or size, the massive majority of businesses have the presence of the leading networks like Twitter and Facebook, and it's safe to say you'll end up with them. And over on LinkedIn, you may need not invest in effort and time except you are in the B2B market. However, Facebook has a lot of competition for your brand to tackle since everybody is there. When you start, gaining audience traction is a struggle and a fact you will have to face.

How to optimize your profile

- **Choose a profile image**. It is not wrong to use a logo for corporate-related profiles. And for brand building awareness with ease, your logo needs to be quality and use it consistently across all networks.

- **Let your profile description be concise**. Inform your followers and fans what your brand's products and services. Be practical and keep away from the muggy catchphrases.

- **Complete updates of your data**. The more data you can give out, the better for your brand. Never leave fields blank. For a potential customer, they could base their buying decision on each of this information. It is when you cannot provide any information that you can leave something blank.

- **Include keywords**. When people are searching for a business like yours and for them to discover your profile with ease, you must include keywords that describe your products and services.

- **Add in operating hours and your location**. For them to get more foot traffic, local businesses must enter the correct hours and locations. In your website, directory listings, and all social media profiles, you must list that information.

- **To fill your profile with content, backdate some posts**. Potential new followers and fans may not want to follow you when your profiles are empty. Your profile may still be new, though, to create an illusion of activity, backdated posts are an easy way. You will be perfectly fine when you make the content, regardless of time, useful, and evergreen.

Building a social media following

You won't have any value for your business from social media unless your followers are targeted. The good news is, you can scale through this problem in some ways. However, these strategies depend on a cautiously created strategy execution with useful and relevant information and stellar content. For customer conversion through a social strategy, engaging with your audience is what you must do.

By targeting only those who match your demographic, using advertising to draw attention to your profile on each social channel is one way to start the machine. Then, to entice followers and fans to share your content with their following, you can begin implementing your incentive-related freebies and the content assets from there, including eBooks and white papers. For your social presence promotions, you can also make use of integrated apps for coupon offers and run contests. On your website, add in your social media profiles links. Also, on your blog posts, include buttons for social sharing on each of them and in the share text, as well as your social buttons. Alert your email list to your social presence if you've got some subscribers for them to follow you, include links. With hope, they will follow you back, for people in your demographic, actively search for them and follow them. Your followers like that you're paying attention, so, be approachable.

How to develop a content calendar

You will need to post regularly to keep that following actively engaged and stay consistent. Though your audience is statistically more likely, at certain times, to respond after seeing the content and you won't see any magic bullet posting schedule. Don't appear always tooting your horn by being a broken record even when you will undoubtedly want to promote your services, products, and content. Doing this means getting your audience unfollow you or to tune you out. If possible, share helpful information you're the users can benefit from other sources while you will create a mix of content that originates with you.

Across all of your networks, you may be tempted to post similar updates. Refrain from doing that. The best way out is to customize the updates with regards to each channel's style and format. You need to adjust accordingly for best response potential even though the style can be the usual one.

Chapter 3: The Need for Social Media Marketing for All Businesses

One of the highly essential digital marketing aspects is social media, and reaching a global audience is one of the incredible benefits it provides. As you can broadcast your product and mission with ease, you may be missing out on an incredible marketing opportunity if you are not applying this valuable source. Here are some of the reasons your business needs social media marketing:

Value-added brand awareness

As productive, stress-free digital marketing channels, you can enhance the visibility of your business through social media. Other people can see how you engage with them when you create a social profile for your business to get started. Then, you can boost your brand awareness significantly when you apply a social media strategy. The social media marketing efforts of about 91 percent of marketers heightened user experience and improved the recognition of their brand significantly by spending only a few hours per week. It is no doubt that your business will have a profound benefit when it has a social media page, and in no time, your business can enjoy a broad audience with regular use.

Cost-effective

The most significant way to effectively cut costs for an advertising strategy is social media marketing. For nearly all social networking channels, you can sign up for free when you want to create an account. And to have an idea of your expectations, always start small if you decide to use paid advertising on social media. You will have the ability to budget for other business on a bigger scale and marketing payments. Also, when you are cost-effective, you will get a higher return on investment. It will be possible for you to get a return on investment on the money you invested and significantly increase your conversion rates by spending a little money and time.

Audience engagement

For interacting and engaging customers, social media can be an excellent way. You will have more chances of conversion with your audience when you put in more effort into your communication. For you to cater for the interest of your audience with ease and know their wishes, it is with your target audience; you will need to set up two-way communication. Moreover, some of the means you can use to convey the message of your brand to your audience and win their attention are engagement and interaction. Thus, exclusive of any difficulty and in real terms, you will establish your brand as it reaches more audience.

Enhanced brand loyalty

Your customers can easily find and connect with your presence on social media. There's a high probability of upsurge customer loyalty and retention when you connect with them via social media. Brand loyalty and customer satisfaction typically go hand in hand as practically any business's main goal is to develop a loyal customer base. You need to jump into increasing a relationship with your customers by engaging with them most times. For promotional campaigns, social media tends to be a viable channel as it also serves the purpose of introducing your products and services. For your audience to communicate directly with your business, it is as service channels that they see these platforms.

Better customer fulfillment

As a communication and networking platform, social media tends to be quite crucial. For you to enhance the overall brand image, you need to create your company's voice with the help of these platforms. Instead of an automated message, customers will appreciate receiving a modified replay when they mention your brand on social media. Perceived naturally in a positive light, when you make an effort to have your message personalized, your customers will see that you value them.

Marketplace awareness

Instead of communicating directly with them, marketplace awareness is one of the best ways to identify your customers' wants and needs. Also, marketplace awareness is social media's most valuable advantage. You will see the opinions and interests of your customers by observing the activities on your profile that, if you didn't have a presence on social media, you might not know otherwise. Through social media, you can understand your industry quite better and get information as a complementary research tool. Then, to examine other demographics of your consumers, you can utilize more tools when you get a large following.

Additional authority for your brand

Though it all comes down to communication, customer satisfaction, and brand loyalty both play a significant role to boost the power of your business. You will build a positive image in the minds of your customers as you post original content or reply to their queries when, on social media, they see your company posting. It is viable proof to customers that your brand and perhaps you have concern for when you regularly interact with them. Allow your valid consumers to do the advertising for you since they valued your product or service once you get a few satisfied customers.

Increased traffic

Social media also helps get tons of traffic to your website, and it is one of its benefits. For your customers to click through to your website, you are giving users a reason when you share content on social media. And while making conversion opportunities, the more generation of inbound traffic, the more quality content you share on your social account.

Improved SEO rankings

In calculating rankings, one crucial factor is social media presence. SEO requirements are continuously varying when you want a successful ranking secured these days. As a result, regularly update your blog and optimizing your website is no more sufficient. By speaking to your brand constancy, integrity, and validity, you will achieve that as a search engine receives your brand signal when you share your content on social media.

It is both creativity and strategy that social media marketing requires. Its essence cannot be overstated even though it may appear quite overwhelming. And with approximately 97 percent of marketers using social media, it means it is so vital, and with the use of social media for their business, 78 percent of salespeople outsell their peers! Also, the benefits of social media go beyond increasing sales.

However, social media marketing benefits can be so obscured that not all businesses know about it. Indeed, about 50 percent of small businesses are not utilizing the power of social media to promote their business. That's an alarming figure. And with an additional 25 percent having no plan of using social media in the future either, it is even more concerning.

Clearly, for those that are struggling to get started and others that are seeing the benefits, there is an apparent disconnect. You need to keep reading if you are struggling to get started. How you can build your business through the help of social media marketing is what you are about to learn. You will soon learn some benefits like:

- Promoting your products and services: you are investing in marketing all because of this.

- Increasing your traffic: you will be able to increase your traffic tremendously when you link your social media to your website.

- Brand awareness growth: you will get the words out to the world about your product and mission through social media marketing.

How to Increase Your Brand Awareness Using Social Media

Brand recognition creation

The utmost essence of the marketing goal of any business is to gain brand recognition. It is as simple as buying from a brand they recognize for consumers. And you can get useful and secure branding through social media. Much more easily and quickly, social media can make people know about your brand, which gives it an edge over traditional media. Furthermore, irrespective of people not knowing of your brand or product, social media gets your audience looking at your brand. One of the crucial elements here is to take careful note of your cover photos and profile. You need to be strategic with the way you place your logo for maximum brand recognition creation. Ensure that it is not distracting or overwhelming.

You must ensure that you have good representation when it comes to your brand's visual elements. You must keep your social media profile clean and neat. And without being overbearing, you can place your familiar logo on your cover photo and also profile image. Your logo needs to connect your idea of what your business does with your logo to make your cover photo quite useful.

Create a brand conversation

Generating discussion around your partners, products, and brand is what a strong social media marketing strategy will do. On your social media messages, when audience comments, engage with them. Let them see that someone is behind the brand. They will feel more like a valued customer with a healthier awareness of your brand when you ensure that they don't feel like they are talking to a robot. You can create conversation naturally by focusing on content sharing. Here are a few ways to go about it:

- To other brands that you work or network with, give shout-outs

- Request for products feedback

- To get your audience actively involved, let them reply to open-ended questions you ask

Utilize social listening for audience connection

When you monitor social conversations about specific topics, you are engaging in social listening. You can discover if your target audience is following some trends and have an understanding of what is significant to them through social listening. Then, doing this can aid your content creation to address the pain points of your audience when you learn the things with which they are struggling. Also, you can identify the languages and tones that your audience is using.

You need to see what people are saying in your industry when, doing social listening, you make it your daily habit.

Tell your brand's story

For your brand to share stories and also your brand's mission, social media can be an excellent tactic if you are using it. Your brand's image will have an abundant impression through powerful stories. With regard to what you believe will be highly effective, these stories can be extensive or simple. The people that make use of your products or services are the ones you will share their stories. Then, share it when you receive great feedback. You need to know that for you to gain positive feedback, your product must be valid, and sharing it will spread the message.

For improvement, collect data from audience research

Typical of social listening is audience research. However, it is more focused on your specific product even when it is the keywords your audience will be using is what it searches. And to gather this information, you can make use of social media. To observe the insight and the reach of your entire posts, both Twitter and Facebook allow you to do that.

Enter the profile that you have access as an admin when you want to view the insight on your Facebook page, and beside your cover photo is where you will find them. As for Twitter, at the bottom of each tweet, you can view every tweet's insights.

Make followers happy through the provision of exceptional customer service

Now, through social media, customers expect brands to take care of their needs. Between your customers and your company, you can build meaningful relationships through a customer service substantial investment. Customer service challenge is still as tricky as it had before with social media. You can get instant customer feedback and interaction through social media. And almost immediately, customers can get the response of businesses. It is imperative to have a social media customer service strategy when nearly half of the customers in the U.S. utilize social media to inquire about products and services.

Between teams for customer service and social media, it is essential to preserve robust communication if you have separate groups for both. Doing that, while using social media for the provision of customer service, your units won't get tangled up.

Develop loyalty with customer

It is free for you to build brand loyalty. When customers enjoy brands, they interact and follow them. 53 percent of customers are likely to be loyal since they follow your business precisely, and that is interesting. It is an apparent direct correlation: versus your competition, you will likely be the choice of the people if they follow you. Furthermore, you will see a boost in your traffic through them if they are loyal customers. Below are some ideas to keep your customers happy and audience:

- To make a long-lasting impression, give out cheap things like hats, lanyards, sunglasses, shirts, patches, and stickers

- To propel your audience to respond, ask open-ended questions

- To your customers through social media, offer promo codes for discounts

Building a Social Media Marketing Strategy

For 2020, have you squared away your social media marketing strategy? Well, no one will blame you if you have not because social marketing's vortex year is 2018. With regard to its privacy concerns and algorithm changes, the public shrouded Facebook with controversy. Even with more than one billion users on its platform and also rolling out a whole slew of business features, Instagram finally came to its own. As the quest for real brands increases for customers, launching seemingly controversial and conscious campaigns, several brands got bolder.

With an orientation of purpose, you can deal with your brand's goals with the help of a social media marketing strategy. For you to optimize your results, have the audience's engagement, and identify your goals, below are some of the crucial steps for your social media marketing guide:

- Optimize as you assess your results

- Make timeliness a top priority

- Content curation and creation for engagement

- Competition analysis

- Most essential metric establishment

- Audience research

- Set actionable social marketing goals

Tackle your main challenges with set goals

Out of social media, the things you want at large is what you need to figure out. In your industry, could it be a larger voice share? Or is it more of social-savvy consumers? Either way, don't count it as a sprint, but marathon when it comes to social media planning. Setting actionable goals must be everything you always strive to achieve. For example, it may not happen if a million new followers on Instagram are what you want. However, in a way that is both affordable and reasonable, you can have your social efforts scaled by tackling realistic, smaller goals. And from social networks, you will deal with your budget; everything will influence your goals.

Model of social media goals for 2020

You can conquer and divide some of the actionable goals below for your brand.

Brand awareness expansion:

Avoid publishing promotional messages alone when you attempt to create lasting and authentic brand awareness. Instead, content that, ahead of the hard sell, takes care of the pains of your followers and emphasizes your personality needs to be your focus.

Accomplish a more exceptional quality of sales:

Without listening or monitoring specific hashtags, phrases, and keywords, it is almost impossible for you to dig through your social channels. You will discover that it is much fast for you to reach your core audience through more efficient social media targeting.

Drive in-person sales:

For brands to drive in-store sales for social media marketing strategy, there has been a hunt by some brick-and-mortar companies. To entice folks to see your business is social media promotion of your brand enough? And are you informing your customers about some events in your stores such as your store's action shots and promotions?

Improve ROI:

It is not by accident that social media ROI tends to be positive. You can help keep down your creative, ads, and cost of labor by reviewing your social accounts. Out of your social spending, squeezing way more will be the end result.

Build a loyal fan base:

Is it content generated by the users that your brand promotes? Without any initiation, do you get a positive reaction from your followers? When you make an effort to encourage your customers to post on your behalf, they will become not only your new content sources but also your best cheerleaders.

Industry's better pulse:

What is working for your competitors, and what are they doing? To drive sales and engagement, what is their strategy? The way to place your company on and also off social media is an analysis that can help you to understand better.

For you to have a clear understanding of which platforms to deal with is the combination of these explicit goals. Instead of having several objectives that will results in eventual disruption, keep your social media strategy simple when in doubt.

Audience research

For marketers, a dangerous diversion is to make assumptions. And there's no need of worrying for you, courtesy of social media analytic tools and demographic data's sheer wealth. Already out in the open are the information you need to prompt your strategy for social media marketing. An excellent example is today's demographics of social media. There's no fluff about the demographic data also. What types of content to publish and which social channels your brand must attempt is what these numbers speak directly. Some takeaways are below:

- Perhaps with the regards in part to their user bases with a high-earning, prime places for ads are YouTube and Facebook

- Instagram's majority of users are below 30 years of age, indicating content that is eye-popping and bold

- On Pinterest, believed to enjoy social shoppers' value of highest average order is the fact that women are more than men

- More than what is on Facebook and Twitter, the well-educated user base is LinkedIn, which makes it a place for industry-specific, in-depth content that could be quite difficult

Can you imagine how this goes down?

And what about your customers even when, into each platform, you get insight through the demographic data? That means, on social media, before you can genuinely identify the demographics of your customer, you will need to do further analysis.

Create your most significant metrics

You need data-driven for your social media strategy no matter what you are selling. The importance of the metrics for your social media needs to be your focus. If they are not resulting in meaningful sales and engagement, shares and "likes" will be futile metrics even though they are nice to have. If you have nothing to do with them, then what good are your million followers? For you to build lasting, meaningful followership relationships, engagement metrics are vital. While it is excellent to have likable content and a broad audience, for 2020, you need to watch some of these additional metrics closely:

Reach:

Your post's number of unique readers is the post reach. Across social media, what is the reach of your content? Is your content reaching the feeds of users? For you to track reach is arguably more essential than ever talking about the organic algorithms that are ever-changing.

Clicks:

Your logo's click rates, click on the name of your brand, or content. For you to have a clear grasp of how your marketing funnel drives users, link clicks are quite critical. For you to fathom the factor that inspires users to purchase or motivates curiosity, it is essential to track clicks per campaign.

Engagement:

The division of the number of impressions with the total number of social interactions. It could be a good ration out of total reach to see who interacted for engagement. You will get more information about your audience's inclination to relate and how well they perceive you.

Hashtag performance:

On your side, what hashtags created the most engagement? What hashtags that people use most? Which hashtags have the most connection with your brand?

Paid and organic likes:

These types of likes have definitions through organic or paid content, more than just standard likes. That is the reason

Facebook Ads become some brand's favorite. As a result, you will find it much harder to gain traction for channels like Facebook. However, it is not quite as challenging on Instagram to earn organic likes.

Sentiment:

The reactions of the users to your hashtag, brand, or content is this measurement. Is there anything offensive in your recent campaign to your customers? What are the hashtags' types of your campaign with which people are connecting? It is good to identify conversations by people through deeper digging.

A valuable strategy of social media marketing has its roots in numbers. You will have it circle back around to your original goals with those numbers that you must put into consideration.

Research your competitors

You need to be abreast of what your competitors are up to ahead of content creation. Your analysis needs to be surface-level for you to do this. For some brands to dig deeper into the numbers of their competitors, third-party competitor analysis tools are also quite essential for them. You will get direct information about your strategy for social media when you look at the presence of your competition. It is not to steal or copycat the ideas of your competitors with the goal here. Instead, it is about how you can adapt your campaigns accordingly when you have determined what is working for them.

How to identify your competitors

A simple Google search can be a straightforward approach to dig out your competitors. For you to see who shows up, search your most important industry terms, phrases, and keywords. For example, to investigate, "handmade natural soaps," if you sold various soaps, would be the right keyword. Through ads and organically, the people showing up in your space needs your attention, excluding Bath & Body Works and Amazon. Then, social media active users among them will be the next thing you want to search for. In this situation, with a thriving, active social presence, a smaller operation is Wild Soap. As a result, you can track them as an excellent candidate.

For your brand to quickly compare its performance and those of your competitors, tools for social media competitive analysis can be handy after identifying some of your industry rivals. You can see their Facebook postings and against yours, contrast their Twitter engagement. On Instagram, to rinse, repeat, and use strategy optimization to identify their content tagging.

Curate and create appealing social content

Content is the core of your social media marketing strategy. Based on your brand identity and your goal, you must have had an excellent publishing idea at this point. Also, the networks which you want to cover are reliable to you. But the content that needs to be posting could still overwhelm you. There is a lot to mull over when talking about discovering the stability between personality and promotion and picking the right creative. In a time where 46 percent of users indicate they will renounce an overly promotional business, the pressure is undoubtedly on brands. Also, as for brands that share too much irrelevant content, 41 percent of users confirm they would unfollow such a brand.

You need to start with 2020's best practices and social trends so you can have a clear understanding of what you must be publishing. For your social media marketing plan, as you put together the content piece, take a look at any combination of the following.

- Bust or video content

- User-generated content

- Build content themes

Chapter 4: Creating Social Media Marketing Plans for 2020

At the core of most marketing strategies will social media marketing be, and the world of marketing will witness significant changes as we inch closer to the end of the decade. But, in 2020 and beyond, how do you triumph in your social media marketing?

In a time where every single soul is online, social media marketing tends to be crucial to any strategy of marketing. Indeed, the figure of 3.196 billion of social media users globally is staggering. As it is now, social media will never be the same. Today's counts will be tomorrow's trends. For you to have a permanently current strategy for social media marketing below are simple guides, you need to make:

Social videos widen the scope

As well as for marketers, one of the things the audience loves is videos. Through the human brain, well retained, engaging, and self-explanatory are videos. By 2021, the video will have internet traffic of global attribution of 80 percent.

Live streaming events

Pulling along with marketers and consumers alike are backgrounds of products and services, product launches, and 'how-to' videos. Videos will grow into vastly peculiar aside from using it for conversions and brand awareness by 2020. Some of the things for which marketers will make use of videos include:

- **Online shopping visual content** – with their e-commerce strategy, marketers will have social videos in syndication with shoppers having a preference over other ad forms for how-to videos, video ads, and short-form videos gaining traction.

- **Networking** – building a loyal follower community for marketers by leveraging the opportunity of users consuming more videos for education and entertainment.

- **Individual communication** – walking you, for example, through the features of a device with personalized videos

The development of VR and AR

The tremendous opportunity for innovative marketing is to generate outstanding encounters for customers and engage them. With AR, Augmented Reality, for real-life experiences, can have mind-boggling layers of depth through the use of VR,

Virtual Reality, to bring a simulated environment or a faraway event to life. With the push of features on social platforms such as Amazon or Lens that aid the virtual clothing for users, Geofilters by Snapchat, Oculus Rift Glasses by FB, to boost their advertising revenue, marketers will incorporate many of these elements to engage and entertain their audience.

Consumers search for products through social media

Customers of today are informed and tech-savvy. As a recommendation, a survey carried out indicates 84 percent of participants putting their trust on reviews found online. Therefore, a lot of factors need to be put in mentions, likes, shares, reviews, and so much more by marketers. Most likely, your customers are searching for the popularity or social recommendations about your product, while advertising is all you're busy doing. For your audience to discover necessary information about your brand, social media will most likely be the first place for your prospect look. In the event of searching the product online by customers, social networks are where 28 percent of consumers look, as a report from Globalwebindex indicates. For product searches, there is a possibility that social media would probably outmaneuver search as social media platforms continue to receive traffic of users.

Buy button integration for social commerce

To provide users using a call-to-action when they see you via social media tends to be the next logical step. With the provision of a breezy, smooth shopping experience, users can enjoy the commerce platform on social media. With a conversion optimize button, the marketer's ads can get enough supplement. With this, they won't be any requirement for app download or visiting a website through the buy button integration. This trend can indeed increase rates of conversion and add value even though it has not caught up yet.

Maximize sell game

Also, for offline games, online games have been a magnet for people. Candy Crush, Clash of Clans, Pokémon Go, and many others are so popular. Games are widespread across most demographics, with the age group 25 – 44 is 54 percent of gamers, 70 percent of women and 66 percent of men hooked to mobile games. To make sales in the process, educating their customers, and brand awareness, making thrilling games, gaming apps for ads could be another investment for brands.

More significance for insights

From the efforts of social media marketing, there happens to be no data shortage. You can collect valuable insights into understanding the journey of customers better and their behavior by monitoring preferences and usage as well as pulling data from different platforms as more crowd congregate on social platforms.

Unique content

With virtually every individual quickly producing, out there, there is plenty of clatters. For every individual, now is the need to create such customized content. It appears possible even though it may seem determined with emerging technologies and an astonishing data quantity you can now access. Based on their preferences, clicks, and likes, customizing a newsfeed for users is the next step for some social media platforms. Marketers can create ads and content handpicked for a person as this trend continues to grow.

Niche platforms for targeting

The platforms that cater to mass audiences are Twitter, Instagram, Facebook, and some others. However, to make a connection with a specific niche, platforms like LinkedIn make it easier. Marketers will have the ability to focus on a particular user base as niche social platforms gain popularity.

Power of AI

Right now in vogue is Artificial intelligence, AI. Artificial intelligence can help you automate and engage your customers, offer personalized recommendations, perform predictive analytics, and help with repetitive, mundane tasks when you combine it with machine learning. Along with social media data, marketers will leverage AI to:

- Identify issues of business

- To craft relevant and personalized messages, use ML algorithms

- Make provision for customer support with the use of chatbots

- Offer product recommendations

How You Can Be On Top of Digital Marketing Game in 2020

Soon, the expectation of digital marketing is to snowball with the changing trends and advancements in digital technology. Amazon, an e-commerce player, prioritizes marketplace. Google, the giant of the search engine, emerges with new approaches by rolling out algorithm updates to give importance to customer engagement and experience as well as leverage the intent of buying and enhance customer experience with the shopping tab. At a rapid pace, Vernacular Searches and Voice searchers are growing, and through 2020, an exponential development will happen to the trend.

By 2020, 19,000 Crore is the approximate reach of digital advertising with growth at 32 percent CAGR, as the ET survey indicates. Also, by 2020, spend on digital media will explode to 24 percent from the present 15 percent, as data suggests. And by 2020 as well, there will be an increase of spends share of three verticals with 25 percent for Search, 36 percent for Display, and 38 percent for Video in the CAGR growth.

Now, how do you want to be extraordinarily smart in 2020 with digital marketing?

Marketing and technology integration

End-to-end consumer experience preparation:

Merging technology with their marketing insights is quite essential for brands. And for their brands, the realization is dawning on the organizations about the essence of consumer experience and also the significance of it. For them to provide end to end customer experience by emerging with digital marketers, there will be a crucial purpose for the advancement of AI.

Marketing automation:

It is just personalized and modified content that some people prefer. Marketers must have a sense of providing more customized and personalized content with many insights available from the vast amount of data and the recent increased streamlining of data. Thus, with regards to the merge between marketing and technology, an exquisite change is what marketing will undergo, and its automation will evolve.

Invest in VR/AR:

For consumers to enjoy improved services provided by marketers through technologies and to develop strategies, they are pressed by the VR and AR use. For customers and business organizations, in the process of information collection, the advance transformation will happen. And for the enhancement of the overall online experience of customers, marketers will have to bring in digital innovations.

AR ads on Facebook:

Facebook is expected to be the future wave as it has heavily invested in AR. Based on their patterns of purchasing, it will be possible to make product offerings and have interaction with their target customers for organizations. With ads for augmented reality feed now in place, advertisers can have their products displayed through a new platform provided by Facebook. The ads through AR feed will aid better conversions for business organizations, and it will even become a more interactive experience with online shopping.

Evolution of measuring store visit online:

To decide the number of footfalls or store visits accomplished by promotions on the internet is the major challenge for web-based brands. With the provision of accurate information, a digital tool is all that business organizations must invest in with the use of digital marketing proficiency.

Marketplaces' distinct budget

In digital marketing, like a giant, Amazon will emerge:

Last year, ad revenue of the quarter by quarter, Amazon has a growth of triple-digit in its record. For a client of any consumer product, it is an immense platform due to the users' high buying plan. To change the landscape of digital marketing as it shows how committed Amazon, it is also evolving at a rapid pace.

Participate in Amazon automation tool:

Within the next twelve months, nearly two-thirds of advertisers on Amazon are either expected to use automation tools for ad campaigns or using it. As Amazon ads will increase their market share, in the next couple of years, significant growth is expected of the market.

Amazon SEO optimization:

For online shopping, of over 56 percent of consumers, Amazon is the first choice as per industry insights. And if other platforms will be their choice, 51 percent first crosscheck with Amazon. By the end of 2020, 10 – 15 percent is the expected increase in this search behavior. In the strategy of SEO for any e-commerce, this situation reflects upon the essence of directly researching keywords using Amazon and the essence of using 'Amazon optimization.'

Google Shopping expert

About everything Google Shopping related, it is advised to stay alert in digital marketing space, in Google Shopping, profound changes are expected. In online shopping ads vertical, as the next big thing in prediction is Amazon, the inroad into the piece is Google Shopping. To choose from a more structured shopping option it provides, across the sphere and through organic searches, Google has already started rolling shopping tabs. As a result, preparing heavy shopping in their digital wing is essential for digital business organizations.

Major changes control and adaptation

Voice search:

For marketers, there will be a massive rise in voice-based advertising as the devices for voice-based AI rise in demand such as Google Assistant, Alexa, and Siri is on the rise. Products' size and name are enough for people to order them when using these products. By 2020, voice searches will make a considerable trend shift, and every passing minute, it is on the rise.

The supremacy of video:

At an all-time high is the viewing quotient of the video, with a viewing time of video content or TV average 30 hours a week. The shift in this huge trend takes the form of video watched on TV and mobile. Being consumed at an all-time high rate in the content of video channels such as zee5, Voot, Hotstar, Netflix, Amazon Prime, a surge in them has occurred. It will be crucial with the use of advertising on video content channels or mobile-based for digital marketers. New realms of opportunities are now available for digital marketers and by the service providers to leverage the Internet.

Mobile ads yielding for native:

Sixty-three percent, on mobile, is the native ads estimate prediction of the mobile display ad revenue. Display ads dominant are native ads with this clear indication. More than any other display ads, higher engagement is visible as native ads incorporate relevant and exciting content.

Customer personalized engagement

Focus on customized and private messaging:

With the trend of the private messaging set to continue in upcoming years, brands are shifting their focus on their customers getting more personalized content. In digital marketing, current evolution is advertising on the private messaging app, and it is with a storm that the space of digital marketing will receive it.

WhatsApp advert:

At the moment, WhatsApp is the social messaging app trending at the moment, and its vast reach is still unexploited. Recently, they launched the latest WhatsApp TVC and on WhatsApp, with ad budgets shift, and as a mass reach marketing channel, it is expected to continue to grow.

Social media strong presence:

As compared to the web or app, social media tends to grow, according to 63 percent of the marketers in one of the studies. Among the customers, for brand connectivity and brand awareness creation, it is vital to have a stranglehold on social channels. As they are adding several new features to YouTube, Instagram, and so on, social channels are constantly evolving. Social media is here to stay. Therefore, to have a social media presence is utterly essential for digital marketers.

Major Marketing Trends for 2020

2020 is almost here. And each year, forcing marketers to evolve their best practices are disruptive and new technological innovations. As the only player in town before, digital marketing has now grown into multichannel marketing. Thus, the omnichannel age of today is approaching rapidly. Most business organizations find it challenging to sustain the continuous acceleration of marketing innovation rates. The significant part is there are new opportunities with doing things in new ways. For 2020, among organizations, the major trends in marketing include:

On-SERP SEO optimization

Have you heard results that are zero-click? You have likely seen them. In the form of an automated snippet to the search query to provide the answer automatically by Google is a zero-click result. For example, the result Google generates automatically will be given to you when you put in the search bar, "what is the weather in Texas?" For you to get the results of organic search and Adwords results, you'd need to scroll down.

Also, for queries that are quite long, Google auto-populate search results. And Google may prevent you from scrolling down to see more results since everything has a snippet, from "what is the marketing strategy on social media," to 'what is a cryptocurrency?" What is the significance of this? As Jumpshot data indicates, search results of 61.8 percent are results of zero-search in Google. Consequently, the profitability of more keywords is dwindling. So that Google chooses them over anyone vying for the same spot, brands are not sure how to optimize their content, while it is from a website that ranks anywhere on the first page of the search engine that the automatic snippets sometimes appear. As for any advertisers or businesses that market on Google, this situation is a worrying situation. The only opportunity here is that there will be a massive competitive advantage of on-SERP SEO is for the business that understands it.

Voice search optimization with smart speakers advertising

In recent years, smart speakers' proliferation is another significant development. As Social Report indicated, consumers purchased smart speakers about 56 million in 2018. Though this case appears to be changing, there has been a scarcity of advertising opportunities and smart speaker marketing, even with more households asking questions on Google Home, Siri, and Alexa. For example, shortly after the flash briefing, scheduled morning announcements, users of Google Home got to know that a worldwide ad for Disney's *Beauty and The Beast* started playing in 2017. Though now growing in popularity, at the time, these ads types were infrequent and rare. With smart speakers, there were less invasive, better-branded advertising examples in 2019. You only need to make a 'branded skill' and to advertise on smart speakers; it offers unlimited customer-friendly opportunities. For example, courtesy of the premium tequila maker, with a diverse selection of possibilities, Alexa will respond if you speak at it, "Ask Patron for a vegetarian dinner." According to Digiday, this strategy is effective, and in a month, there is an excess of 6,000 queries that Patron receives. The opportunity here for business is to go for a tone that is customer-friendly in their branded advertising by trying the "branded skill" approach.

Voice search optimization

Advertising on smart speaker tends not to be an ideal marketing strategy for most brands right now. However, what about using a voice search to explore their content optimization? Right now, it is mostly through voice search that Google search queries get 20 percent from people, according to Google. And as Thrive Analytics reveals, between 18 and 29 of ages, users of all mobile are 71 percent, and they utilize voice assistants. For all businesses, it makes sense apart from large companies to start using voice search to optimize their content. To do the trick, conversational content will be effective, and marketing experts have so many guidelines on how to do this. The opportunity here is to optimize for voice search since it is on smartphones that most voice searches happen.

More content and chatbots

Written content is here to stay. With the increased usage expectation by 2020, the written content is the primary throughput for chatbots as, three years running. It will make the leading commercial effect on marketing activity. By 2023, retailers can expect to increase sales by $112 billion and cut costs by $439 billion annually with the growth of AI-powered chatbots in sophistication and popularity, as Juniper networks' recent study indicates. It is quite tricky to see the reason with the continuity of large organizations to invest in more helpful and newer chatbots with such figures.

However, for large brands, chatbots are not useful. For it to help convert visitors into warm leads, a simple chatbot has the benefit of getting questions by visitors answered for any brand's website. The opportunity here for any business is that chatbot will help them cut costs.

As a marketer, you must learn to change as marketing changes. The year 2020 is almost here. And have you reflected on innovative and new ways for your marketing spending? Or how does your brand get the perfect channel for its marketing? Your competitors are already on it! Now, step on it if you haven't!

Chapter 5: Your Brand's Social Media Strategies Success and How to Build Effective Strategies for Your Brand

When you have a strategy, you will do well with social media marketing, which is the crucial ingredient. For the sake of posting, you might find yourself posting on social media platforms when you don't have a strategy. And it will be challenging for you to achieve results on social media when you don't understand what your target audience wants, who they are, and what your goals are. You need to develop a social media marketing strategy regardless of leveling up as a social media marketer, or you want to grow your brand through social media. The way to go about doing it right is to know:

How to create a social media marketing strategy

There are a lot of crossovers when it comes to a social media marketing plan and a social media marketing strategy. How you will get there is a plan, and where you are headed is a strategy. For your social media marketing strategy creation, the 5Ws is one of the easiest ways by asking:

1. Who are you targeting as your audience?

2. Why are you creating a presence on social media?

3. When will it be right for you to share?

4. Where will be perfect for you to share?

5. What types of posts or content will you share?

Having a strategy has another interesting point. For each of your social media channels, you can have a plan, leading to your overall social media marketing strategy, including an Instagram marketing strategy and Facebook marketing strategy. However, your overall strategy is where we will begin this discussion.

Why do you want to have your business on social media?

The very first question that requires your answer is the big WHY.

This fact has a connection with your social media goals. Is it to promote your products and services propels you to be on social media? Or is it to serve your customers or drive traffic to your website? Generally, you can have nine social media goals, and they are:

1. Listen to your brand's types of conversation

2. Intensify press mentions

3. Provide social customer service

4. Build a community around your business

5. Boost brand engagement

6. Grow revenue through sales and signup increase

7. Generate new leads

8. Flood your website with traffic

9. Increase brand awareness

While the goals above are general ones, it is okay if you probably have more than one social media goal. Mostly, except you have a team where different purposes can be tackled by several people, it is useful to focus on just a handful of goals.

Who is your target audience?

Your target audience is the next thing you need to consider once you have figured out your WHY. You will be able to quickly answer the following questions on when, where, and what you are going to share when you have a clear understanding of your target audience. For example, a company could share tips and tricks on web designing on its social media if such a company knows that its target audience loves to read about web designing. Building marketing personas is a great exercise you have to put effort into here. For your marketing personas building, there are several ways of doing it. Use the 1H and 5Ws again for this approach.

- How do they consume the content? Like watch videos, read social media posts, and so on.

- Why do they consume the content? Like staying up to date with something, becoming healthy, getting better at their job, and many more.

- When do they look for the type of content you can provide? Is it during their daily commute or weekends?

- Where do they usually hang out online? Is it Instagram, niche platforms, Facebook, etc.

- What are they interested in that you can provide? Like information on new products, case studies, educational content, entertainment, and so on.

- Who are they? Their education, salary, gender, age, job title, and so on

It is not indeed from scratch that you will likely start. You most probably already have a good sense of your target audience if, for a while, your business has been running. So that you can use it for your future reference or share it with the team, what might be helpful is to write it down.

What type of post or content will you share?

The type of content to share is what you will come to mind with a question like this. For example, is it images or videos that you will like to share?

But wait!

You may want to step back and reflect on a higher level since the marketing strategy for your social media is the bane of discussion here. "Theme" might appear a more precise word rather than the content types you will share. Let's discuss the themes of some brands:

- A brand that shares memes mostly on the profile of their Instagram is a couch brand called Burrow

- Another brand that shares high-quality and outdoors editorial content on the profile of their Facebook is an adventure and outdoor brand called Huckberry

- Another brand that shares photos from their products and customers on their Instagram account is an underwear brand called MeUndies

Having more than one central theme, you might have noticed that about the brand, if you check out the above mentioned social media profiles. And without being seemingly unfocused, to keep your audience engaged, it is perfectly fine to have a few themes as you can share different content. At this juncture, it can be useful as it is where you know your target audience quite well. You may want to consider the questions below as you analyze the personas of your marketing:

- What do you do to work out their challenges and goals?

- What challenges and objectives of your target audience?

Newest fitness gears updates will its target audience goal for fitness accessories and apparel brand. On the profile of its social media, as a result, will it features the latest products sharing. And addictively promotional isn't right. Because 70 percent of American teenagers totaled 8,600 that participated in the Piper Jaffray survey indicated that, through Instagram, they preferred to get new product updates from brands. Your target audience consideration is the key to succeeding with this.

Where will be perfect for you to share?

The platform for content sharing is the subsequent phase. Do you want your brand, in other words, present on any social media platforms? You need to understand that having a presence on every social media platform is not necessary for your business before the discussion continues. Better content creation will be easy with more time, and you will have a better focus when you are on fewer channels.

A quick note here: since, when people search for your brand, on Google search results on the first page, you would always show up. At least, on the Big Four, it is wise to have a complete profile, which is LinkedIn, Twitter, Instagram, and Facebook.

Again, it comes handy here by understanding your relevant customers. Are your potential customers active on particular platforms? What is the reason for their visit to that platform? When their brands have new products or they are free, for example, young adults and teenagers might like to scroll through Instagram. Your brand's "X factor" is a different factor you need to consider. Do you have skills in writing, videos, or photography? To specify content types is what particular channels impart themselves. For example, Medium is a platform for articles, YouTube for videos with long-form, and Instagram for photos. However, with the evolution of social media channels to deliver virtually every content type these days, this particular case is a minor point.

Digital Brand Strategy Creation for Optimal Growth

By 2020, what will be the most crucial factor for brand building? For a practical growth guide, developing a consistent digital brand strategy is the simple answer. Your personal brand or business gains to be long-term with this rewarding yet challenging process. With more tangible things, some of the general increase, apart from ROI, that you will see include:

- Advocacy

- Loyalty

- Brand awareness

In the competitive advertising and marketing of this age, consider the above three priceless assets. For anyone to remember your brand, impressions of about 5 to 7 can be all it takes. Besides, there are bed impressions. The key for people to have a good opinion about you is to have a solid brand-building strategy. After all, your brand's perception of a customer is the definition of your brand. You need to know that on social media, one brand gets followed by 50 percent of consumers. With your end-user in mind, this stat of social media entirely defines the essence of the optimization of your campaigns even though your digital brand strategy will encompass a number of elements.

So, how do you go about it?

Well, you must have a clear grasp of your digital audience as well as your brand vision. As they evolve, your digital brand strategies can be successful when you have a handle on these two things. With which all the campaigns of your brand are designed, success centers around developing a consistent process, despite the inevitable change. And for high performing strategies implementation for execution, this process is what your company will use.

As you read on, you will have insight into:

- Brainstorming a digital brand strategy plan

- Creating a guide for the growth of brand strategy

- Essential keys to branding your business

Now, let make a deep dive.

First, it may be wise to examine the basic definition of online digital branding and brand strategies.

What is a brand strategy?

A complete blueprint is a brand strategy, and as long-term development, its focus is on your brand's emotional impact, consistency, and purpose. And when a unique identity is connected with the competition, the brand strategy defines how you differentiate. Here are some of the specific goals that brand strategies have their base:

- Encouraging advocacy and loyalty

- Using interaction to develop a positive perception

- Increasing overall awareness

What is a digital strategy?

The aspect of the plan for general marketing is a digital strategy. In the form of sales and leads generated, it has its focus on the entire mechanisms that propel the growth of the business. And it is through online channels that this process occurs. The tools to get you there is a digital strategy, even though to position your business is the aim of brand strategy. Some of the components about the plan of a digital strategy are:

- Paid advertising, PPC

- Email marketing

- Social media marketing

- Website user experience

- Content and SEO marketing

It will then be logical for us to answer the question that follows as we put the above together, which is:

What makes a digital brand strategy?

It is everything that a digital strategy comprises that a digital brand strategy encompasses. However, it is on the principle of your brand's goals and guidelines that it is founded. And it is in the brand strategy's overarching that, indeed, those principles are. It is when you are branding your business effectively with the awareness of the essential keys that it could sound simple. Well, let's continue to dive deeper.

The keys to branding for business

Ahead of attempting to create a digital brand strategy, every company must review these main components of branding. You can define foundational pieces of your business with the help of one of the elements. If ever, these things will change rarely. Also, for you to develop effective processes, these cornerstone qualities guide your brand. Aligned with each component of branding for business, make sure you have an excellent answer to the critical questions:

- Brand recognition

- Benefits and qualities

- Brand voice

- Competitor analysis

- Target audience

- Brand purpose

Brand purpose

What propels you to do what you are doing?

Indeed, you will know the why behind providing your products and services and also understand them when you outline an answer. Under an umbrella, the determination of your brand purpose may include:

- Tagline

- Values

- Vision

- Mission

Target audience

For whom are you providing your products and services?

You will not have a positive impact on business goals with everything else you do to build your brand if you don't understand your consumer. Without trying to be everything to everyone, your consumers' behaviors and buying habits, as well as the specific lifestyle, is what you want to understand.

Competitor analysis

How do you stand out from the crowd?

In the marketplace, the process of reviewing your competitors is part of what you will need to spend time to do. Doing this, you can pinpoint how you will do something better or differently. In your industry, take a look at the key players. For those that you'd like to model, which are benchmark brands, and others that will compete with your brand, you will need to study them.

Benefits and qualities

What is the uniqueness of your business?

For the products and services you provide, the chances are that you are not the only business offering them. However, your brand is the only business with your skill, team members, and specific process. You must determine what makes your business distinct. For example, the reason you believe you are the most forward-thinking, or the most valuable or reliable.

Brand voice

How will your audience receive your communication?

In the same way, on multiple channels, people will recognize your brand image when, in a cohesive voice, you maintain consistent messaging. It is illogical to be formal one time and conversational or fun in another. So they can get to know your brand, you use your voice to convey the brand's message to consumers. You must always remember that how you want people to perceive you is your brand's voice. By developing it carefully, make sure you are giving off the right impression.

Brand recognition

What are the ways you will use for your consumers' engagement?

Through engagement, here is where you will put everything into practice. And it is through consistency that you can build recognition and rapport with your audience. Through brand recognition, you can build trust with consistent engagement. Make sure your engagement is both meaningful and memorable. In many ways, you are going to engage your consumers digitally. As a result, to improve your chances of success, keep the above keys to branding in mind when developing new campaigns.

Brand Development Strategy Planning

Process development is quite similar to developing a brand strategy plan. You need to refine as your brand development strategy boasts of the creation process behind it when it comes to growing your brand digitally. Planning is the sum of everything. As your company grows, creating the plan so you can use and reuse it is the digital brand development strategy's first element. As you execute effective marketing campaigns and scale, your brand standards will enjoy efficient maintenance.

It is typically this way you may want to perceive it:

Even when the design is unique, to curate a new build, an architect uses a similar process. Or: at the restaurant, though the dishes may vary, it is in the same manner for a busy night that a chef prepares.

Even though there may be a change in the platforms and content, with the use of a similar effective process, your business can develop new marketing campaigns. Everything is done countless times, before execution, creation, and development. Hence, as soon as you are prepared for the marketing campaign execution of your second, third, and fortieth, you can streamline that cyclical effort with the help of creating a brand strategy process.

Elements of the digital marketing campaign

In a digital marketing campaign that is strategically designed, you will always want to include some of the things like:

- Analytics reporting process

- Process of paid advertising

- Ongoing SEO implementation and auditing process

- Social media engagement process

- Content strategy by platform

- Brand voice guidelines

You may include more or cut down from it with regards to your digital marketing budget and the size of your company. In addition to the above-listed items, a larger company may implement:

- Social media customer service process by channel

- Influencer management process

- Process of cross-promotional and partnership

- Social media content processes and curated content, blogging, for SEO

- Email marketing processes for retargeting, segmentation, design, and acquisition

So, to manage this process, what is the best method? For marketing and brand development strategy guide, you can use these five steps:

Discover branding key elements

What will help you, as earlier discussed, the new marketing campaign will get the help of the essential components of your branding. Also, as you develop a new brand development strategy process, consider the following factors:

- How will you engage with your audience meaningfully?

- Where does your online community consume content?

- What is your digital brand voice?

- In all of your marketing campaigns, how will your mission, after defining it, be ever-present?

Team responsibilities definition

From the individual contributors to the executives, it will help everyone when you have clearly defined roles. Your upcoming marketing campaign engagement will determine each person's responsibilities. Those roles could include:

- Quality assurance

- Reporting and analysis

- Advertising manager

- Designer

- Content creator

- Project manager

Develop your refining and brainstorming process

The actual refining and brainstorming process is the next thing you need to do. For example, you can have a PM compilation and report, a refinement period, a review, a kickoff, and a concluding duty for a two-week project.

KPIs and goals determination

Without first defining what success looks like to you, tracking your campaigns' progress may not be feasible. For business growth, S.M.A.R.T. is all you need to create initially. And for regular tracking, creating indicators for essential performance must be your priority. Here are some KPIs:

- Cost per acquisition, CPA

- Conversion

- Traffic

Indeed, based on what is essential to your business goals, in your digital branding strategy, there are several other metrics you need to include. For grouping them, you may use the following categories:

- Website

- Social media

- PPC, pay-per-click

- SEO

- Email

- Marketing

Reporting template creation

Your analyst can utilize your KPIs on the failures and successes of each campaign, to report back once you have determined your KPIs. Ideally, so you can make adjustments along the way in your strategy of the digital brand, you will use the KPIs to track progress throughout the marketing campaigns. Doing this will have the highest possible return generation as well as helps optimize your efforts. Your brand will possess a valuable data bank by keeping a record like these reports. You will know what is working and what is not. Also, you will know how to capitalize on the ever-changing trends.

Chapter 6: How to Increase Social Media Followers to Strengthen Your Brand

If we tend to discuss the real definition of social followers, we can say that it represents a user who chooses to see all of the posts of another user in their content feed. For online businesses with a social media presence, their primary objective is to get their users to follow their accounts. There is a form of the news feed on Facebook, Instagram, and Twitter, which delivers content to its users. By platform, the content of news feed varies, and from other people whom the user has chosen to follow, they consist mainly of images, articles, and posts.

There is a distinction between shares and likes. A follow has an expression of interest in receiving constant updates, while the indication that people find value in an individual post can be shares, retweets, and likes. With the audience, a follow indicates a higher level of engagement, which, more than other engagement metrics, gives it more value.

How follows work

For commercial purposes, businesses use "like a Page" or "follow" for users of Facebook. People open social media accounts that falsely claim to represent well-known individuals or businesses. To add a layer of security, Facebook utilizes a verify function so they can combat it. The process is quite different from Facebook when it comes to how follows work on sites like Tumblr, Instagram, YouTube, and Twitter. Any user can follow any other user since, by default, all profiles are public on those platforms. Through news sites, blogs, and searches, users can find brands and people to follow.

Indispensable Ways to Grow Your Brand's Social Media Presence

It is a way of connecting with people that social media started. However, for businesses, it has turned to a go-to destination for them today. As a result, you can't afford to not have a presence on social media, whether your business is online or offline. Well, how can you ignore them when billions of active users log on Facebook and Instagram every day?

For your business to target and reach customers, you have a bunch of options on these social media sites. These days, to engage with their audiences and grow their social media presence, nearly every brand has a social media account. To drive valuable traffic and conversions, social media helps you improve your brand awareness. When you take time to enhance your brand's social media presence, you will undoubtedly reap the many benefits of social media.

Ways to Grow Your Social Media Presence

In the digital world, when you attempt to amplify your product marketing strategy, social media can be a great way to accomplish that. For you to boost your social media presence, there is the availability of several tried and tested methods. To implement these methods, let's take a look at them.

Set your goals

It is essential to have clear goals in mind ahead of getting to work on improving your social media presence. For the things you want to achieve, you must have them in mind. And before you start the other steps of your campaigns, you must execute it. You might be wasting your resources and time if you don't do this. How each social media platform works is essential for you to know, and as for the audience you are targeting, you must have an idea of them. You can use interests, locations, and demographics to target your audience.

As a brand, to know which direction you are moving in, you need always to set precise targets. This process could be to generate leads, boost engagement, grow followers, and increase brand awareness. In the long run, you will be able to increase your social media presence and measure your success when you have specific goals.

Create a great profile

You must check your profile first when you are about to implement your strategy. You need to fill all fields applicable to your business and complete your profile. One of the things required for you to grow your social media presence is a complete profile. A short bio that tells your story is also essential. So that it may help to drive traffic to your website, use a few relevant keywords while writing this bio. Use tools like Google Keyword Planner or KWFinder to find such relevant keywords.

Your display picture and cover photo are also essential. Have them handy. Apart from being attractive, these images must have your brand's logo on them. They are the first things anyone visiting your social media profile will see. For viewers to navigate away or scroll down, the deciding factors are your profile images. As a result, to increase your social media presence, they play a contributory factor.

You will improve your brand's credibility once you have completed your profile with essential information. People will begin to trust your brand further if they can find relevant information whenever they visit your profile. Chances are people who may not get to know your brand if there is little or no information. And this scenario can hamper your chances of improving your social media presence.

Follow relevant accounts

When people know that your brand is a legitimate one, you can then start growing followers. Then, you can follow other brands and accounts of real people to help prove your legitimacy. You must make it a point of necessity that these accounts should be relevant to your business and brand. Doing this will increase your social media presence and establish your authenticity. You will get to improve your credibility further when several of these brands and personalities follow you back.

Interact with your audience

With the use of helpful content, the next thing is to start posting on your account once you have gathered some followers. However, your social media presence will not grow by only posting content with media or links. To grab your audience's attention, you have to start interacting with your audience. On your posts, when your follower's comment, reply to them or respond to their posts. The process is to have your brand connected to your audience and also for you to connect with them. Then, your audience will have the desire to know more about your brand when it connects with them. For you to read more about your posts, your audience will then the visit site as their connection to your brand continues to rise. For example, on Twitter, there's a bit frequency on customer interaction for Starbucks. With that, their social media presence gets improvement, and they gain traction.

Understand your audience

You will have to understand your audience's needs as you start interacting with them. You can take your interaction with them to another level by making it more personal. Your content can have a specific element in it to benefit your audience when you know what they want to read or see. Then, your social media presence will get a boost as they engage with it often when they can relate to the content better. Also, there will be room for bringing them to your business or website when you can fine-tune your content. As you continue to present your audience relevant content, you will solidify your understanding of their needs further down the line.

On your website, put follow buttons

Now your site is getting more traffic, and it is essential not to waste it. It is useful for your social media presence growth, or you can gain valuable followers on your social media accounts. One mistake several brands are making on their website is not putting buttons of their social media on it. You can increase the number of followers and your presence on social media with ease with these buttons. At locations that it will be easy to spot them for your visitors is where you will put them. However, you may end up putting off your visitors when, all over your website, you have them, you have gone overboard with it. On your website, placing them on the upper-right side is a good practice. Let each button has its definition because doing that is essential. And also, between the follow and share buttons, try to make a clear distinction.

Link your website and profiles

It is also vital for your social media accounts to have to your website, all links such as Twitter, Instagram, and Facebook. It will be secure when you do this, for a brand to engage your audience with more information. Also, you will gain more presence on social media and increase website traffic when you do this.

Conduct events

For you to spread your brand, events can be a great strategy. You can make use of it on your signage or printed materials, social media accounts, or even hashtags, and your audience will notice, and also events will get tractions with them. At events, you may have a few social media accounts and hashtags promotion by getting as creative as you can. You will grow your social media presence as your social media profiles will get traffic by doing this.

Profiles sharing

By simply sharing the social profiles of your brand, you will enhance the presence of your social media. It is with those known to you that you will share your social media handles. However, go about it not in a forceful way and refrain from spamming them. On social media platforms, they will be aware of your presence, and then they will spread the word to families and friends.

Use hashtags

Under one roof, you can bring similar content through the use of hashtags. You need to learn how to incorporate some hashtags on your social media accounts whenever you post something. People will know about your website as well as your presence on social media. Mainly when using Instagram and Twitter to post, hashtags matters a lot. However, don't overload hashtags on your posts and overuse them. You will only end up harming your presence on social media since your posts will look spammy. Branded hashtags are also useful. These types of hashtags have in them your slogan or the name of your company. You will continue to grow your brand's social media presence and increase brand awareness when people use these hashtags to create posts through your encouragement.

More networks for leverage

Among the popular social media networks, including Google+, YouTube, Instagram, Twitter, and Facebook. However, on the other social media platforms as well, you should try to boost your presence on social media. You can try out Tumblr, Foursquare, Pinterest, and some others. What about social review platforms and sites for social bookmarking? As much as possible, make an effort to increase your presence on social media.

Emails and social icons incorporation

About your social media accounts, a great way to spread the word is email. It is possible that every month, your subscribers are getting multiple emails from you. Your readers may be prompted to check out your social media profiles in your emails if the icons of your social media are present. Again, doing this can boost your social media presence since you are getting more followers and additional eyeballs. Ensure you include your social media handles in your newsletters if your audience is getting them regularly. Even if you send it out via the mail, you can still do this. What about having all your social media handles on a card you are slipping? The presence of the social media of your brand will be improved when you do this.

Give out perks

People love freebies. And to be your followers is the reason you are giving them when you provide them with a freebie. Your brand needs to draw your audience while choosing a freebie even though you can choose anything to be a freebie. Let your audience have a discount code or a free trial. You will see that people can spread the word when they motivate them about you apart from helping to engage your audience. Again, you will be improving the presence of your social media as it helps your brand grab more eyeballs.

Engage, engage, and engage!

When you engage with your audience, you will gain their support. And using engagement, make it personalized. When you to know what your audience expects, there will be engagement with them from your brand when they follow your brand. You may want to make an effort to respond to them whenever someone comments on one of your posts or posts about your brand. There are other ways as well that you can engage with them. Encourage them to participate in contests, quizzes, and polls that you set up. Your followers can also get your engagement by utilizing Instagram Stories.

To build long-term relationships, inform your followers by sending out a clear message to them that you care about them when you actively engage with them. This makes them loyal followers of your brand, and your brand will have their complete trust. You will see them recommending your brand, since they are now loyal followers, to their friends and families. In turn, you will continue to nurture the presence of your social media.

Content optimization

On your social media platforms, the search engine can see virtually everything you post. This translated into search engines like Google listing your posts. So, whenever possible, incorporate some relevant keywords, as a practice, into your posts. And for the right keywords on Google, you will get visibility for your posts. Similarly, you can make use of the previously mentioned keyword research tools on Google to research the search terms of your followers. Then, you can grab the attention of relevant users by using these keywords in your posts once you have identified relevant keywords. Ultimately, you can improve your social media presence as you start getting more visits when, and in the search engine results pages, content from your social media ranks higher.

Locations of your brick-and-mortar can be effective

Also, you can utilize your physical store for your social media presence traffic if you do have one. You can grab eyeballs on your social media handles inside an attractive poster you put inside your store or on the window of your store. Your social media accounts will be seen by the people when they arrive at your store. Also, many more people can get your attention when you place a poster on the window if your establishment has one. Even with your social media handles on the poster, include engaging visual content. Also, to grow your social media presence and get more attention, you could have your social media handles printed on your business cards or receipts.

Post regularly

On social media, it is generally a great practice to post periodically. Your target consumers will notice you quickly, and they will notify you. However, equally important is the content posting frequency. Your audience can think that your social profile is not active enough and might start losing interest when you post too rarely. In contrast, they might feel that you are spamming them when you post too often. Before posting consistently, absolute stability is all you need. As a result, your presence on social media presence will get a boost when, at a regular interval, your audience gets information. For you to have optimal times for your posts, you can also schedule them in advance if needed.

A personal touch is perfect

Make an attempt while addressing your audience not to use generic words whenever you are replying to them. Instead, address them with their names and attempt to have your messages personalize. Also, make an effort not to make use of template-built responses as you keep your answer genuine. Each time, tailor your response. Your audience will have a sense of intimacy with you when you do this. You can damage the reputation of your brand because, to people, machine-based messages are quite annoying. Alternatively, your presence on social media can get healthier improvement since people will always appreciate a genuine reply.

Deal well with complaints

On your social media accounts, take your customers seriously anytime they complain. As well as in a professional manner, let it be as soon as possible for you to respond to their concerns. Stay away as much as possible from automated responses such as 'emails us if you have any questions.' Instead, in a personalized way, answer each complaint and take time to have their concerns examined. You must always have it in mind that your business can get a recommendation from your customers to their friends and families. And it will help you if positive feedback is what they give you. Ensure that you remain that way, even if the input of your customers is not polite. Remember, people will always have a brand that cares about them as their favorite.

Also, your customers' interaction with your brand will be noticed by others. You may get some new customers, thereby increasing your presence on social media if you give them a positive impression, just as much as the similar opposite impact with a negative reaction.

Request from your customers to share

For your branded hashtags to be shared in their posts by your existing followers is another great way to attract more followers. You will increase your presence on social media, as this strategy will attract more attention and eyeballs towards your profile. To encourage your followers for branded hashtags sharing, offer an incentive to them for the best results.

Separately manages networks

You need to handle each social media channel differently, even though they serve a similar purpose. Across all platforms, using the same content could be a grave mistake for you. Take time to have each social media channel treated separately. And in different ways, optimizing every one of them will be easy. As a result, your presence on social media presence will have substantial growth with this optimization. Certain discoveries that are quite interesting came up from a study which indicated that there is 21 percent higher engagement with Tweets' hashtags that one or two number than one with new hashtags. Also, according to other research, there are significantly higher interactions with posts on Instagram with 9 hashtags. You can also drive the highest engagement when, in a day, you have 3 posts on Twitter, according to another study. Similarly, in a day, after two posts, the engagement drops drastically on Facebook. On Pinterest, daily five posts are ideal for the best results. And on Instagram, 1.5 times daily. Your presence on social media will continue to increase when you follow these best practices.

Chapter 7: How to Find and Use the Right Voices/Tones for Your Social Media Marketing

On the social media sphere, voice is one of the several ways to be prominent, apart from amazing visuals or killer content that marketers often overlook. Virtually everyone wants authentic communication on social media, not some brand that talks at them as if they are signs of the dollar. Since it is not the same conception with other online strategies of optimization, it can be quite challenging for your social media marketing to get a voice. Voice is far from being a design element you can tweak or a statistic you can track. It is much more than that. You can practice and place rather than analyzing and tracking. If, as a brand, you plan to interact online and figure out your voice for online interaction, read on as you will soon discover what works best.

How tone and voice differ

Tone comes to fore when, within social media marketing, you dive into the ocean of discussion about voice. Most times, people use them interchangeably since both of them are together. And so far you have the definitions, with this regard, it doesn't matter what definitions you give it. But with a direction that has a concise description, you will be better off knowing where you are headed. The definition that makes a distinction between tone and voice makes the most sense and below is the breakdown of the differences:

Voice:

In an adjective, this is the description of the personality of your brand. For example, brands can be professional, cynical, positive, or lively.

Tone:

Your brand's voice's subset is your tone. Based on factors such as channel, situation, and audience, your voice's flavor is the addition of tone.

Mainly, there are several tones that enhance your brand's voice and one voice for your brand. A mission statement is a voice while that mission's application is tone.

A formula of four elements is a different approach when it comes to voice. We can break down voice not only to tone, but also purpose, language, and character:

Persona/character:

Does a sound connect with your brand? With specific suitable attributes of how you like to sound online, here, this identity can get enough elaboration if you picture your social brand as a character or person.

Tone:

How do you describe your brand's typical vibe?

Language:

In your social media conversations, what use of words connects with you?

Purpose:

In the first place, what is your reason for being on social media?

You can have your brand's overall definition with the help of these four points collectively. And into each area, to gain insight, it is quite useful to experience, and these same parts and ideas are connected to the process of social media voice determination. We understand that tone signifies the particular voice implementations, and your brand personality's overall defining sound is the voice.

The importance of tone and voice to your social media

The essential factor that makes tone and voice matter is that your natural conversation engagement is smooth as your brand gets a sense of human. You will see your marketing effort being made by others for you with a voice for social media marketing. Does it sound like a fairy tale? Well, here are the things you need to know:

1. Delight your customers with voice cultivation

2. With essential new content creation, your brand receives a positive talk by delighted customers

3. Delivering the message of your brand for you through prospective and other customers get this content

You need to grant an engagement of genuine personality when your brand can have a face, in other words. It isn't information people fancy most times, but connection. You will ultimately get a flood of devotees that your brand will quickly have growth by them when you do this right.

Finding your brand voice

Voice can have a precise definition with social media as the analogy being a massive barbecue and cocktail party. Rather than asking questions, telling stories, listen, and relate to people, you would not want to encounter a person at an event and tell them that the discount of your product is 20 percent. Don't go about telling people about your low prices. Instead, in virtually every of your social media marketing, it is crucial to identify the uniqueness of your voice.

It is adjectives you're searching when voice is what you seek. Primarily, your voice would have been found when there's the best description of your brand through adjectives. You can figure it out with these methods.

The three Cs of brand voice

When you start examining your conversation, community, and culture, for your brand, you can begin to develop a voice.

Culture:

What is your brand's representation? From your competitors that have their eyes on the same audience, what is unique about you? What is special about your culture, and what qualities of yours are unique? And for your voice development, a pillar is needed.

Community:

You can get help to speak easier to your community and with them as well as reveal how they speak through listening. It will be easy for you to connect favorably with them when their language is utilized.

Conversation:

The key here is authenticity and personality. Does your conversation need additions? The picture will begin to clear to you about certain places fit for your voice as the offer you can provide comes to mind.

Probing rightly

Details and information gathering is the next thing you will do once, courtesy of the brand voice's three Cs overview; you are indeed in the right direction. So, to start asking the question, where is the great place? Here are some of the points for you and your brand to create your brand voice:

- How do you want your customers to think about your company?

- Does your personality correlate with other brands? What are the factors of similarity?

- Describe what the character of your company is not in adjectives

- What is their relationship to the consumer if a person was your brand? A dad, teacher, friend, coach, and so on.

- What is their personality if someone happens to be your brand?

Research using the right individuals

Your valued customers, your team, and also yourself can take up your record of quizzes and questions. To these questions of voice, the answers will likely have insight with uniqueness from each group. Consider diving deeper with this process with customers, and for your brand's voice has further traction, draw on their social media interactions. Use some of these things to evaluate their social interest:

- The other companies they follow

- Their most frequently shared messages

- How other brands receive their messages

- The tone they use to speak with one another

New prospects need to be polled. After a few days of purchase, follow up with them with an email to thank them for buying your product and using the best description about your brand experience, in all simplicity, ask them to specify the precise adjective. For your brand's unique qualities and to obtain valuable insight, you can get that from clearly several people. The adjectives that define your voice is all you need to settle on by using all possible data.

How you can translate your voice to your tone

Now, you have to decide on the tone you will use in various communications, with adjectives in tow, by working out your brand voice into specific ways. As we discussed earlier, the tone is where you apply voice with the individual instances like the interactions, the channels, and the conversations, while how you communicate on social media is the voice. To identify your tone, you will have to work from a template in a straightforward way, especially one that shouldn't write to keep with your voice but about the ways you should, the one that has you thinking. After coming up with content type, you can fill in the details in a template that require a specific tone like this:

- Tips: explain best practices of writing for this scenario

- Write like this: give a brief example of how the writing should sound

- Let the tone you use be: adjectives are quite necessary with how you sound since, in this situation, it describes that

- Feelings of the reader: when they are in this tone scenario, what is the feeling of the reader?

- Content-type: what are you writing?

In practice, they can look like this:

- Tips: use plenty of questions. Never sound authoritative. Invite others to learn and discover

- Choose this way to write: "did you know to help people work less; they invented an 8-hour workday? You can get the story here."

- Work on your tone to be: approachable, clear, informative, helpful

- Reader feelings: engaged and eager to discover exciting information and content

- Reader: marketing professionals, potential customers

- Content-type: tweets

Tips for finding your social media marketing voice

You can have a better overall experience for your brand and your customers when you develop a voice for your social media marketing. Not only will the payoff be big, but it is also through an endearing way that a voice helps you connect with your audience. For you to have an idea of where to start in developing your brand voice, the examples and methods above should do the job. And as you keep on searching, you can also tap from some of these ideas.

Use openness and transparency in your marketing

As you are coming up with your social media marketing voice, it can be a massive asset to have openness and transparency. This type of marketing is unique for starters. You can stand out in a crowded field of brands when you take up the idea of sharing the intimate details of your journey. Also, you will communicate with confidence when you write with transparency and openness.

Market your company as if you were marketing a person

Instead of being unique, businesses have a reputation for being generic. As a result, your brand can gain a significant advantage when you market with the perspective of an individual. In practice, just as how consultants, freelancers, contractors, and other people run a social brand, this process would look the same. Apart from being spontaneous and flexible, these people communicate with followers and fans on a one-on-one basis. Indeed, your brand can take a similar way to the market. Your brand can also do everything an individual does. For a social media voice, you can open up several new options when you think from this perspective.

Be consistent and authentic

You may want to have a second look at consistency and authenticity after you have identified a voice and tone for your brand. Below, you can lend from some of these useful ways to describe these values:

- Without being forced, your tone must be authentic

- Inconsistency must be avoided. In a copy that otherwise feels casual, never attempt to interject sudden moment of cutesiness

- Any effort to be funny must be stemmed. Not only will they fall flat thereby embarrassing everyone, they rarely come off as amusing

- Business and context must be your watchword. Never burden those on their mobile devices or others who are in a rush with your thick tone.

Simple Ways to Define and Maintain Your Brand Voice

You showcase your brand voice anytime your business posts on social media, in a conference lecture, updates website copy, or launches an advertisement. And how well you developed the voice of your brand in the first place has its dependence on if you can maintain the voice of your core brand. Needless to say that it is useful to strategize as you define your voice, typical of modeling various logo designs of your business. And without any content, everyone would recognize your logo logically. However, for most brands out there, that is different.

For brands to help distinguish themselves from every other brand, on channels such as social media, they must have a reliance on building a brand voice. But, without scraping all your copy and ads, how does this fall on your accomplishment side? The simple answer is to get your team together. And you can maintain as you define the voice of your brand with the following simple steps:

Strengthen the beliefs of your brand

Are you a funny brand? What will you expect from your customer's perception of your brand? Does your founder or CEO repeatedly say something? Having a great idea is quite excellent; these questions can be quite challenging. If not, you can get clear answers from your leaders as you start from scratch. So, reinforcing your beliefs is essential during your brand voice definition. Therefore, from brands, the most sought-after behavior for consumers is honesty. And from snarky attitude to a bit of wonder, is the slightest favorite of consumers' behavior. Though being snarky can indeed convert customers. Primarily, on social media, by giving followers responses, several brands see plenty of engagement. However, do your brand beliefs match up with this messaging and tone? It is a parallel experience creation that your brand needs to focus on. And across posts on social media, advertising, and content, you will create a similar experience when you maintain your fundamental beliefs. It is through your marketing funnel that you will drive people with the help of these recognizable actions.

And from the side of the customers, they create expectations. You may likely become unreliable if your messages have mixtures. You need to know that annoying behaviors and bad experiences drive the loss of followers on social media for brands. So, across all channels, promoting a similar message, your brand voice does that, and you start by reinforcing your core values.

Your ideal brand voice needs a thorough outline

It will be a smart choice to outline and dissect all your variables if the voice of your brand is all you are still fully deciphering. And it becomes easier to develop Instagram posts and tweets when the communication of your brand is familiar to everyone. Has it occurred to you that because they were embarrassed, a brand losses followership of about 71 percent of consumers? Apart from that, information on brands is not relevant and has had 41 percent of consumers unfollow them. Though the act of balancing can be tricky for a brand to keep customers informed while happy. This means, right from the beginning, a clear voice is a must to maintain for you. Otherwise, your customers will run off after you might have upset, confuse, or annoy them. For a concise plan of your brand, try out these few exercises:

- Detail your social colloquialisms and jargon: on subjects, does your brand speak frankly? Does your use of professional or relaxed jargon have any clear perception from your audience? It may not do your brand any good to have someone posting colloquial and casual language on your social media while another uses professional buzzwords.

- Ensure the strategy of a social customer: when an annoyed customer punched you on Instagram, do you know what to say? Is your customer service number engaging them, or if it more than just a 'sorry to hear that'? Make sure your goal is similar to your interactions and responses, and for questions that come up on social media, your team must be prepared to give the right answer.

- Storyboard your voice: for a writer to develop a character in a script or story, storyboarding can be an excellent method. Find out who your brand wants to be and the end goal of your brand, as well as everything your brand does and doesn't like. Then, you will have more precision when you are defining your voice.

Avoid bait and switch communication

You may send your customers, with a different language, down your funnel as you speak to them one way. This technique might appear obvious. For a sponsored video, article, or other paid content, brands have made 66 percent of people feel deceived, according to a report. You need to stay away from bait and switch methods as, using paid content, your customers can feel quite cheated. For example, you must keep the messaging consistent and clear across other channels if you are using Facebook for a significant sales event promotion. Also, ensure your audience knows about it if your business believes in making products or offering the crispest materials in the U.S. If you promote organic or sustainable items, for users to discover your product information, make it easy for them. For whichever social channel you choose, utilize content on social media that is easy to digest, reliable, and relatable to reinforce your brand's beliefs. From in-person sales to online interaction, brands that attempt to acquire customers have these attributes.

Scrutinize the engagement of your audience

You are pushing your brand voice anytime you upload a video or update status with a post or reply to a message. You must maintain that brand voice when your brand receives users with concerns and problems on social media. As a report from Oracle indicates, for users to get a direct response to an issue or question, brands get the interaction of 43 percent of users on social media. It is so logical. Nobody has the time to speak to a representative by waiting on the phone, and people want brands to prioritize their concerns. You can seek a social monitoring tool to aid your attempts if it appears like too much work to reply to all of these conversations. Also, let customers see your genuine impress when you monitor and listen to your messages. Increasing availability and actions can have significant rewards, while response rates change per industry.

Discover the most highlighted places of your brand voice

You must recognize most places in your company people highlight the tone of your brand even as it is smart to know your brand's tone. You will have increased influence when, through the right platform, you use your brand voice. On social media, the voice of your brand is highlighted on a few familiar points like:

- Visuals: in visual, you can detect your brand voice. As such, ensure that your visuals lead back to your brand.

- Bios: the best place to showcase your brand voice is your social media bios. It merely needs to be YOU and not stern or humorous. Make sure your bios are well-written because this is how many consumers will first see you.

- Direct messages: you must ensure that your direct messages are answered with the utmost care, talking about the emphasis on social customer service. Relaxed text or DMs with jokes could standout if your brand voice is supposed to be professional and trusted.

- Instagram captions: using things like emojis, there's a chance to use creative captions for your audience to get close to you on Instagram. To showcase the creative side of your brand, indeed, the place is Instagram. However, make sure any documents or all components on your company's website match your captions.

- Call to action: like everything else on social media, your call to action needs to match the same brand voice. You may put off your readers when you switch tones with your landing pages or CTAs. Your brand's beliefs must match your CTAs. And what one-to-three words can do will quite amaze you.

- Replies: just as other essential messages, all brand replies must have the same context. You will know the exact tone in which to reply to any comments on social media when you determine the voice of your brand.

Make your brand impressive

It can be quite tricky to stand out on social media with several fusses. Your customers can flock to leave you when you create a forgettable or lousy experience, which can be a lot easier. However, the interactions on social media can get more comfortable when brands develop and stick to a brand voice. Learn to have a keen foresight of how people see your brand and work on promoting your brand voice.

Chapter 8: Social Media Content Creation and Sharing

So many people have been there. Their piece of content created is nothing less than perfect, and with every certainty of getting a buzz around it, they hit the 'publish' button, waiting for the surge of insane traffic. But there is an issue. There no trickle of traffic.

As you must be aware, content marketing's most laborious part is gaining people's love to talk and share your content after reading it. Most bloggers fail as a result of this one main reason. Necessarily, you will have to struggle with content marketing's promotional aspect. For you to get people to share, read, and discuss your content on social media, here are a few ways to do that.

How your content can get engagement

Can you pinpoint how you decide to peruse a piece or not while browsing through a website, social media news feeds, or a magazine? Does the article length, caption, the writer, or the picture hook you? Is it the visual element of it that draws you to read it? The thing is, not a soul will read your write-ups if it has an awful caption, no matter how good your content can be. For you to ensure your headlines are magnetic, check out the tips below:

1. **The double whammy** – you can create the double whammy effect when you use them in one headline or combine a few of the elements below. For example, you may write your headline like "How to Double Your Daily leads with These 5 Simple Steps."

2. **Evoke curiosity** – to make people click through and read your content since they are naturally curious; you can encourage them by making your headline a question.

3. **Mistakes exploitation** – you can create a headline about your mistakes or other people's mistakes so others won't make the same. Writing about mistakes can indeed hook a lot of people since people make mistakes.

4. **Appeal to emotions** – another great way to draw the attention of a reader is to spark an emotional feeling within your headline because we are all humans.

5. **Leverage laziness** – you can leverage laziness within your headline because people don't like working. For example, you can start your headline like 'the lazy man's way of...'

6. **Urgency can be pretty good** – you are more likely to get people to read your content when you tell them that to act on your information, they only have a short window.

7. **Put people over search engines** – if it makes your headline dull and boring, it is not a good idea to add keywords to your headline to make it more search engine friendly. Don't think about the search engine while writing it, write them for the people.

8. **Stats are better than opinion** – use data within your headline if you have it that backs up your main point.

9. **No need to reinvent the wheel** – "List" and How-to" headlines have so much attention with people. So, even if they seem played out, use them.

10. **Where is the benefit?** – Content that teaches people something gets their attention and share. With your headline, let people know what they are going to learn in your article.

Hopefully, you would have got some point here to craft an excellent headline for your content to engage with people. It is time to focus on how to get your content shared now that engaging it with people is clear to you.

Social Media Content That Will Give Your Brand Greatest Value

Posting valuable content is all that you need to do to succeed in any social media strategy you choose. With all the social media marketers' success factors, you want followers, shares, likes, retweets, and virality. Then, it doesn't even worth it to keep trying if this activity is not in the promotional criteria of your social media management. So, you need to ask yourself, how do you get that type of love, and what content on social media do you need? More fundamentally, how do we get significant value with what content?

With regards to engagement, KPIs, ROI, and revenue are what we mean by 'value.' It is in a way that makes your ROI is substantial that you will want to spend your content marketing money. And that is an essential part of social media. So, here are some of the content that can give you great value:

Infographics

The form of content that is most socially shared is infographics. The virality of infographics is than documents and presentations, according to the Slideshare report. In the history of humanity for the studies of the incredibly vast social sharing with over 100 million articles data crunched, large numbers of shares are attributed to infographics, claiming the high rank. Infographics are indeed engaging. Infographics make sense because it is faster than words for humans to process visual information. For the brain of a human, looking is easy, and it is hard to read hard. To trick the brain into reading, an infographic utilizes the influence of content that is appealing visually. Besides, with pictures harmonizing of content, we tend to understand it better. No wonder kids have so much love for picture books. However, it is similar for adults as well and not just the kids. Pictures boast of preference from the brain. The lesson here is: you will get a mutual share from the social world when you share infographics on social media channels.

Interactive content

All the age is interactive content. There is a new trend against the form of social media content of static process-it-as-you-read-it by the industry of content marketing. Instead, better engagement content is produced by know-how content professionals. A quiz is an excellent interactive content. Also, quizzes are content with a form of two-way. Instead of merely consuming it, people perform a task with quizzes. Besides, sharing the results of their quiz is one thing people love. The quiz was the content that got the most shared in 2013, not an article, according to the Atlantic report.

So many reasons make interactive content valuable. The old ways may be all you need to revert to when interactive content is all you post.

Content that induces positive, strong emotion

People may not share your content on your social media quite much if it doesn't spark the feelings of the people. Posts with high shares have an emotional value that is quite high. Though there are a bunch of emotions, and you may be wondering how to get more shares with what emotional response type. Well, people get inspired to share due to the happy emotions. In the shared social media content, there is a connection with positive emotions and also "positive ratings" as well as "positive feelings." As a result, irrespective of the niche you are, have your focus on emotion if you genuinely want activity on social media that has value. The universal language emotion evokes is similar response everywhere.

Obviously, with regard to the demographic makeup of your audience, your emotional language will vary accordingly. However, your brand will see valuable results through emotional language in social media.

Integrate images into content

Content that is image-rich shouldn't surprise you when it gets incredible shares on social media. According to some compelling studies, on Twitter, tweets with images has 150 percent more tweets, and on Facebook, photo posts attract more than 104 percent more comments than the average post. Photo posts receive 84 percent more link clicks than other text and link posts. This goes with the earlier infographics mention. The brain and eyes have an attraction for the content on your social media, share it, and absorb it when you pepper it with images. You will certainly increase your value if, on social media channels, you maintain a steady content rich in the image output.

List posts

It is with regards to many blog posts types that content marketers' classification of content and a standard arrangement includes:

1. Why posts: these are articles that explain things or situations, usually consisting of the headline, the word 'why.'

2. What posts: general information and news articles

3. How-to posts: how-to-do-something content with extensive explanation

4. List posts: content with a specific number of points

List posts come on top, as indicated by Kagan's data. The data tends to be reliable since the researcher analyzed articles totaled more than 100 million. Also, list posts topped the spot with a similar study by Hubspot. With a 2.5 percent less variance, social traction's most reliable is 'why' and lists posts, with fair shares per month of about 21,000. Also, with a small claim of 22.45 percent, list posts triumphed between why posts and list posts. As some writers point out, it is natural to engage with lists for the brain. As a result, getting benefits on social media from shared list posts, people will always engage and share it.

Newsworthy content

More than any other article types, news articles get more social shares in raw numbers. However, as it happens, breaking news as a source can be hard. Those that can do this are these businesses types which are:

1. Niche sites with a constricted slice of news as their focus

2. Big news organizations around the world with reporters and journalists

Instead of as-it-happens breaking news, the focus is on content with a profound long-form for most content-producing businesses. Producing news articles shouldn't be your focus if the news industry is not your niche. The reason? With regard to the industry analysis, the awful players are the "what-posts" or news articles. The only news articles that are shareable are entertainment, technology, and news verticals.

The low-performers on social are the what-posts as they are risky, as Hubspot indicates:

- With total shares of 17.88 percent, the lowest traction on social are the what-posts

- What-posts, with 13.45 percent high variance, were the riskiest format

On social media, what-posts can have value if you are in tech, entertainment, or news niches. Otherwise, learning to maintain some other method will be better for you.

Strategy to Develop Hardcore Content on Social Media

At a brand's disposal is a highly versatile tool called social media. As an open platform, by one side, it allows for an unprecedented direct engagement. However, full of constant noise, by the other angle, cleaving through can be quite tricky. Within social media, building a base for loyal fans that are circular community's part is the trick. To bring people back again and again, nurturing a sense of belonging is all needed by you. You will need to combine a content strategy even though one way of doing the job is direct interaction.

Content influence

Content is essential, whether the buzzword catch up with you or not. And in return for their interest and support, it is precisely the thing you provide for your followers. Content is the mode to entertain and impact information. While in authority and not only in substance, as a method of building a brand, it is, most of all, the most fail-proof and consistent. For what you would find elsewhere, content on social media is indeed the same beast. Presented for social sharing optimization as equally valuable content, it is just another strain of species. Here are some necessary steps for your strategy for unstoppable content on social media:

Create your audience

First, you need to establish your audience and their needs. The thing is, if your audience is not known to you, you cannot figure out how to create good social content. Part of the strategy for your general digital marketing is targeted audience research, so with your use of the software for the website analytics, you can get some insights. Content preferences, acquisition platforms, as well as basic demographics, are some of those insights. To give you more information, here are some tools with a focus on social media you will need:

- For you to identify the most engaged social media followers of your competitor, Fanpage Karma will be quite handy

- You can gain insight into how their fans receive the updates of Facebook pages and also compare pages with the help of BuzzSumo

- You can get which content from your competitor's Facebook page that their followers engage the most as it also provides an in-depth analysis of their page through BirdSong Analytics. With the software, you can also get their posts' most frequent words, and the time and days trigger most interactions.

Capitalize on some social media keyword research

You will have the power for your content to get honed through keyword research. For your social followers, or prospective audience to have your attention, more specified form of analysis is keyword research for a social keyword is the social keyword. Some of these tools will allow you to have a glance at engaging discussions and viral updates. Indeed, to see the usual appearance of your core terms context, you can simply look it up on Facebook, Twitter, or your chosen network. You may want to check out Cyfe for social media with customizable features if, with several widgets, cheap alternative aligns with you. Their tools for social researching are some of the greatest. For example, for any hashtag or keyword, you can analyze, archive, or import search results. Another relevant tool is Serpstat. As for the core term you're searching, you can identify your target user's several queries using one of its free features. For your brand to address the most specific needs of your audience, this can be significant information that gives you inspiration for a lot of content.

Start analyzing potential networks to focus

Before, during campaign development, the recommendation would have been for them to target a few social networks. Away from a single channel, since most platforms have made expansion, that is not the case anymore. However, there's every possibility that there will be multiple pages on a minor class, and without the force of a team, they may grow their primary social media using one of them. As such, in the beginning, it is good to put work into them as you create profiles on some social media. Along the way, multiple ways of tactics and content on social media can be tested to see, which yields the best results. Though somehow clear-cut, this process is more of several tests. Similar to the way you would when it comes to a feature or design, you may not necessarily need to have networks that not performing well closed. Then, you can use the one that works best as you identify for them, the form, and the use of content that works. As you individualize each platform's audience, several content campaigns for different social media will be your focus to create. For allowing you the opportunity to exploit the platform for something, and something valuable, doing this has the added benefit.

Create a calendar for your content

By now, your plan for content with a great idea should be forming in your head after figuring out people that will read your content and what works on each platform. For all future work, you must draft them, and also, you need to have an editorial schedule. You will discover that the idea is great to incorporate into your calendar a social element. You will have a completely integrated strategy from an incomplete one. Your social calendar can have some of these ideas:

- Events and plans of your company, including company trips, anniversaries, birthdays, and so on

- Concerts, future significant releases of movies, and festivals (for long-awaited events exploitation, gain attentions by cross-relating to your niche when you find memes)

- Business events or big entertaining (particularly those specific to your niche)

- Monthly holidays, including unofficial and weird holidays.

Site performance verification

To consider people coming to a slow loading or broken page after planning campaigns on social media for days be the worst thing in your social media content strategy. This has been the case with the campaigns of some viral content. As you can anticipate, the logbook of social media is the beauty of having more traffic. So, tell them to get prepared. Inform the team at the technical section and make your plans known to them by doing your due diligence. Some of these tips and tools may help down the line:

- The moment your site goes down, use Monitority to get a Tweet, a text message, and an email

- Get a Google tool to validate that your website is mobile friendly and into it, have a content strategy built as you create a native mobile app

- To keep an eye on the performance of a reliable host as you pick it, look for uptime stats tools to do the work

For better results, your social strategy and your content will endow each other as they mesh when you have a calendar for social media.

Incorporate video into your social media content

Seventy-two hours later, about 10 percent may come to people's memory when they hear information. And in the same amount of time, people can retain 65 percent more if the data has a combination of an image. You can increase your click-through rates when your social media has video content, and when you include a video, you can also boost conversion rates on a landing page. If you intend to incorporate your social media marketing, video content, here are some types of video to use.

Hybrid video:

Screen sharing and on-screen video combination is a hybrid video. To engage with your audience, talk directly to the camera and in a presentation, to show relevant information, share your screen.

Animation:

You can make sketch-type video or explainer videos using animation. Irrespective of different video options, animated video is slightly more complicated, and you can use it if you are the adventurous type.

Photomontage

You may want to consider photo montages if you prefer to stay off-camera as a new person to video marketing. To give it a professional feel with an overlay of music and text, you can tell a story through a collection of images.

Screencasts:

Your computer screen video recording is a screencast. For PowerPoint presentations or running online training, screencast can be a powerful way.

On-camera video:

To get in front of a camera and start recording is the traditional way to market with video. For you to give your target audience an insight into your world, use on-camera marketing.

Live video:

For brands to connect with their customers, many businesses are turning to real-time live video marketing since the introduction of Facebook Live. Also, in the last 12 months, Snapchat's popularity has increased dramatically, and Instagram has released its live video features, Instagram Stories.

Chapter 9: Social Media Marketing Mistakes to Avoid

Right now, whether a local small business or an established business, everyone is doing social media marketing. The concept of having a strong presence on social media is what everyone strives to enter. The reason is simple; that's where they can find their audience. However, most marketers make some common mistakes in social media marketing.

- What promises are you making and make not effort for which to cater?

- In social media marketing, what are your competitors doing better?

- Why do a few Twitter and Facebook pages viral, and some are not?

- What causes the failure of some marketing activities on social media?

To err is human, and there is no difference for marketers on social media. Along with your revenue stream, you can experience your followers counting drop when you make too many mistakes. Those mistakes can be avoided as you become aware of them. As a result, in your marketing on social media, don't make some of these mistakes:

Making no plan for a marketing strategy on a social media

Your social media marketing strategy requires a similar approach you use to figure out your business audience, products, and niche. You could be one of those businesses that execute with their solid strategy for social media marketing left behind. It all begins this way: to attract the attention of the people, you dish out great content, load your profile with info after making it, and that is after joining a social media channel, and you left. Typical of a desolate land is your page within weeks of your 'super' launch, with some people getting no responses after they seek answers while many wonder what they are doing there. In the end, a flop show is what your presence on social media soon turns out to be. You have left an essential factor behind, which is your strategy for social media marketing.

You must never let it dwindle even though your plan for social media marketing has built while you are there. For using social media, what goal do you want to achieve? To get followers or gain likes? Why? To supplement a recent sales leads source? For your brand authority solidification? It may not be possible for you to attain it if you don't know your goal. There would be a requirement of marketing on social media such as:

- Team

- Time investment

- Tactics

- Target audience

- Goals

Without giving you anything in return for you or your staff, your hours of productive time can get sucked away by social media. Plan for social media marketing is all that is required of you, and the idea of sticking to that plan is also vital. Also, measurable and predefined goals are essential, and for those goals to be accomplished, you must create plans. That your time is not getting wasted on futile activities, you must set time limits and take steps to achieve those goals.

Audience targeting

The highly essential factor is your target. If you are aiming in the dark, it will hurt your results even though you have been working quite hard.

Social media negative feedback management

This mistake is common in almost all brands. Lame excuses are the common things brands do when addressing it on social media whenever a negative comment pops up. While many apologize, others fudge it. Brand's reputation is important to them, and they fear negative feedback could spoil it. On social media, one of the most considerable risks is this situation. However, improvement opportunities should this be for brands, rather than ignoring or apologizing for the negative comments. One of the high chances provided by social media is to engage the person who dropped the feedback and start a conversation.

The experience of the user that results in the product's sincere feelings is feedback, whether negative or positive. As a result, brands will find it easier to recognize the shortcomings of the product when they get more detailed feedback. To give them considerable attention is all customers want from the brand, especially those who drop negative feedback. Though, brands must meet their needs by doing their ultimate best, particularly when, for their opinions about them, their customers go the extra mile to let them know, and even with the expectations of customers that are constantly changing.

It is indeed the future better product experience assurance that customers expect, not a formal apology. Rather than pouring money into ORM campaigns, brands must learn from feedback as they clean up their acts. Even with that, negative feedback can be that of criticism of the brand, and not indeed a signal of trouble. Those messages still need a brand's reactions instead of censoring such users. As a responsible brand, you need to rescue the situation when you face negative feedback quickly. During a crisis, manage the social media channels through the response team you have on the ground and also take responsibility for decisions. It is essential not to panic or attack the person who dropped the negative message.

Improving Negative Feedback and Managing Crises on Social Media

Amid your fan's upbeat dialog with you and marketing posts that are planned with care, then someone posts negative feedback, and you don't know what to do. There are some negative feedback types that customers can send to you on social media, and some of them are listed below.

Some negative feedback types on social media

To resolve, the stress-free among these types of negative feedback is the problem. It is entirely on the side of the support issue when it comes to the problem, but by fixing the problem quickly after you must have acknowledged it, you will have to keep it from being aggravated. Make an effort to figure out this problem on social media platforms. Then, to an original post, you can then respond to social media after the successful resolution of the issue.

With your products and services, when it is not working for them, the real feedback about what people feel is criticism. If you don't deal with it appropriately or you ignore it, criticism can go ballistic. Inform the complainer that investigation is going on the issue as you examine the issue. For more negatively expressed opinions gathered by your brand, you can set up a suggestion box as one way to minimize the criticism.

When the idea of beating you up is all a person has or is quite pissed off is when the crisis hits. Usually, it is based on the earlier neglect. The first thing you must do is to ensure that someone is not attempting to get you into trouble, and indeed, there is an issue. For that issue, apologize and show real regret if you screwed up. Then, it is crucial to talk to them about your actions on it. This action requires a specific duration, and you must give them a timeline.

Neglecting negative profile comments

More than its fair share, your brand may derail from its campaigns of social media marketing when it ignores feedback. Perhaps your brand thinks it is not a big deal since, from other users, much response may not emerge from the negative comments. However, it would have adverse effects when on your social media profile, others look at it and bump on these messages. Several individuals may not talk about the comment on another platform as they see the review or comment when they look at your social media profile. The damage has been done even though people may not comment when they see something negative. Make comments that will embrace positive Paulines from negative Nancys by responding to your negative comments.

People always like brands that treat them with respect since they are all about social media. Your brand must be personal and friendly and use the sense of as individuals to treat people. You will have great leads and insane conversions if, with people in mind, you approach the activities of your social media marketing. Learn to address the situation and stay neutral during the time of crisis. Against being the scapegoat, strive to get the problem solved and concentrate on what you can change.

For your brand to identify possible complications quickly, check social media regularly. Monitor your brand's entire presence on social media, including news feeds, forums, blogs, and social media platforms.

Deleting or ignoring mentions and comments

More negative emotions will only abound for you and your brand when you neglect or ignore negative feedback. Direct your customers to the appropriate channels for support, answer questions and act on complaints. Be prepared to react as you watch and not all negative feedback that you have to respond to.

Unfavorable comparisons and reviews can be with other brands all the time. On social media, companies are not addressing negative consumer experience of about 58 percent tweets. You will be ahead of your competitors when you give yourself a good reputation, keep healthy follower engagement, and address customer service issues, whether positive or negative. Some of the things you must do include:

- You won't be able to shake the bad reputation you will give to your brand when you delete or react poorly to posts

- Keep your tone polite and helpful as you request from the customer to email or call you

- Never delete any negative comment or mention you receive

Sit back and relax and understand that you have no control over the message. Give your customers and your employees the opportunity of talking freely. And always ensure that your employees do not use your brand channels for personal messages posting. Some of the other things you mustn't do on your brand's social media channels include:

- Never talk down on others

- Do not lie!

- Don't engage in personal attacks. You may not get closer to resolving your crisis by pointing out some of the things the person complaining does not understand, like technology or problem, as the case may be.

- Apologize and show regret. You may probably make the problem worse if you allow your legal department to deal with it. As a result, do it personally.

- Engage in a personal dialogue. If people talk to a real person with a name, they will be will to cool down instead of being eager to beat up your brand.

- Don't argue. If you have no understanding of the underlying emotional issues, you will not win even if all your arguments are based on facts. It is essential to seek emotions firstly.

- Don't hide information. It will and can come out if there is any chance.

- Create guidelines. In the event of a wave of negative conversations on social media like a negative rumor, customer service gone wrong, the attack against your brand, what path of actions will you take?

- Develop a clear policy for social media. Do your employees delete flame comments about services or products, hate speech, threats against individuals, or abusive or foul language?

- Develop fact pages that will provide further information and also about the situation, answer the key questions. When you have your preparation for possible issues, you can create these pages. And don't use the third-party platform like Facebook but your domains when you create those pages.

- Response team. During the crisis, who will manage the social media channels and who will be responsible for decisions? Since it can be slow with the usual confirmation platforms, top-level management is your next solution. What is the worst-case scenario? Who decides what to do with negative comments? What will be your response to negative content?

- Plan for the crisis. How would you react to what can happen? The worst situation is not to have any plan at all, and even a rudimentary plan will help. Stop thinking in terms of the campaign. And on social media, you don't have any end date.

- Don't panic! Face every available fact for consideration.

- Hours not days. You can keep the situation from escalating if you act fast. And from channels to mainstream media, the issue might grow big enough if you act slowly. In different circumstances, what should be the response times?

- Engage as early as possible when you encounter negative feedback

- To silence aggrieved customers, never use legal threats.

- Censorship. A trivial matter could grow into a massive crisis if you censor user content. If it is based on real issues, never delete negative feedback. The problem will only escalate faster when people get angrier for ignoring them. However, on channels, you have no control; it will do so.

- When a crisis arises, to help you, build your brand's authentic fan base

- Be real. It is not a great way to success when you hire an agency to pretend to be your brand advocacy and faking customer interaction.

Having no human touch and a faceless brand

The fact is, people like people, and when you feed them with crafted messages, you will get it quite fast. Communication between people is all about social media. And on social media, you will see a faceless corporation. Essentially, you need to add some touches of human to your social media profile when you are posting. Refrain from responding with your "stock" corporate response when, on your profile, you are following up with a comment. Don't fall into the habit of using a drawn-up message crafted by the PR department and let your personalized response address the complainer. Also, you need to keep your emotions in check during a negative situation. You can indeed resolve some of these situations reasonably. You must tell your customer that you will fix the situation and that it is under control. Tackle the problem rather than blaming others. You must let it go if the sore part is only your ego.

A ticketing system no longer applied to customer service

On social media, customer service, in the past, was only a formality. At present, for cross-selling and upselling, it is like access that brands are utilizing it. The great thing about online customer service is to get pissed customers to calm down and retaining them aside from its sales benefits. The power of customer service power can proliferate tenfold if merged in addition to social media. Typical of getting a proper solution when regular customers call, customers expect their problems solved by the brand when they engage with brands on social networks. For the social media issues shared by users to get addressed by the brand, you can make use of your customer service team to give valuable answers in seconds. With the adoption of the tactical processes such as understanding the customer discovery processes or motivating buyers through influencers by the lead-gen team or the support people, customer service will become more efficient. Since communication on social channels is free, the brand can lower the cost with this model. You can then absorb the customer service standard model into your social media with time.

Too much of self-promotion

Communication and being sociable applies to social media. Apart from detesting adverts, promotional content doesn't augur well with people. You may lose likes and followers on social media if being promotional is all you do. On social media, you must learn to promote with subtlety. Indeed, you need to sell in your business. So, it is not wrong to post promotional material occasionally. However, you will likely get more sales when you intensify your social interaction and engagement more.

Spamming

Throwing links to your sales promotions and content on all your social media networks is another mistake your brand can make. Spammy and automatic links never work, so don't post them. Engage in meaningful conversation and social media is far from being another advertising platform. Avoid broadcasting!

Insufficient interaction

There could be no participation in the conversation with profiles update in some situations. If you don't build on valuable relationships, there will be a decrease in the value of your social presence when you lack banter with your followers and clients. The reality is, social media is about engagement and conversations even though as banner space, you can make good use of it.

Fake followers

The result of no real followers can be of quite less engagement. Just for the sake of looking better, some acquire followers by buying them. Others hold a contest with prizes such as iPhones and iPads, where people who participate are fans of the products they dish out and not fans of their page. They have forged followers as they keep an active page. You will weaken your presence on social media if you engage in this act. Building a network of genuine people gradually is essential if you want to avoid this.

The mentality of the set and forget it

There is no automatic running of your Facebook page. For your brand to create a fan base, a few ways to do that is setting up a social media presence after creating it. Also, you need to update your page by investing in precious time if you want to engage your fans. Your customer's existing relationship with you will affect, particularly some of them your quick response to their questions and posts, and also hurt your brand's fan growth if you ignore this aspect.

Overlooking diversification

What are the types of content you are posting on social media? You will not engage your followers if you have the habit of posting similar content, especially constant self-promotional materials. You can modify the content type you post to increase their engagement like:

- Tweets or shares from other players in your niche

- External content links that have relevance to the interest of your audience

- Your photos, videos, articles, or blog posts

You need to correct these mistakes in your content as you learn from your content marketing mistakes. Crucial to the small business world is the latest update by Google, which values positive and quality user experience. For you to get your brand out into the world, you need to be on top of the game. Still, the improvement should be on companies of all sizes. Everybody makes mistakes. The most important thing is not to repeat the same mistakes as you learn from them. And for your social media marketing efforts, you will start getting maximum results.

Chapter 10: Useful Tips for Social Media Marketing on Facebook, Twitter, Pinterest, LinkedIn, YouTube, Instagram, Snapchat, and Blog

To increase sales and grow their following, both new and established brands are turning to social media to generate leads. And with all the platforms available, using social media to build a brand might appear like a massive undertaking. However, to grow your brand organically as you connect with people is a lot much more accessible than ever with the help of social media. There is always room for improvement, whether, for years, you have been active on social media, or you're just getting started. The use of each platform is different.

Without further ado, to optimize your marketing strategy, let's get on the discussion on the tricks and tips you can implement on some of these social media platforms.

Facebook

Your brand presence on Facebook is critical, as a marketer. However, for your brand to have a uniqueness about it among your peers is increasingly becoming challenging. That is why you have to be intelligent with the way you grow your business and your audience through Facebook. It is not impossible even though it can be a bit tricky. If, in the crowded social sea, you want to stand out, here are some of the smart ideas to help you with your Facebook marketing.

Specific audience target

Some of the exciting ins and outs about Facebook marketing is the ad targeting's level of super-sophistication. You must have formed buyer personas and analyzed your base for customers with the dedication of resources and time. Then, target your products' potential customers by using those personas.

Boost engagement through a simple contest

There is nothing new about Facebook contests. As such, for ad engagement spike on Facebook, one of the excellent ways to do that is to run a contest with an attractive incentive. Your contest doesn't have to be overly complicated, which makes running it a great thing. For example, you can choose a winner at random for a fun trip by merely telling people to have your product with them when they submit photos.

Produce enticing, short video contents

If your videos are not engaging enough or are not short, people on Facebook may not be interested. To be entertained is all users on Facebook want. You need to use entertaining content to grab their interest fast since they are spending their time on it to stalk their friends or kill time. And the video is the better way to do that.

Direct attention in your images with the use of eye contact

From other people, directional cues of others tend to get followed by people. You may find yourself looking sideways if people in a place looks sideways. It is just human nature. To focus the attention of your viewers on a highly essential aspect of your marketing on Facebook, take advantage of this fact. For example, you can have someone pointing or looking at that text if your CTA is strong.

Cloning audience with main revenue-generating

You have the opportunity of cloning your audience on Facebook that is top-performing when you have acquired enough data. You can find new leads by expanding your reach that has similar attributes through an audience you already have using a feature like Facebook's Lookalike Audience. Cloning your best customers is quite pretty much simple for you.

Twitter

In today's society, there is no denial of the essence of social media, and for a brand to initiate engagement, they must be there. Day by day, there's an increase in usage. And out of the 7 billion global population, 2 billion of them use social media. Your brand cannot risk ignoring this fact. And your brand can get a presence with social media that enjoys prominence like Twitter. For your brand to increase sales and traffic through Twitter, here are some ways you can do that:

Twitter cards implementation

An excellent means for you to ensure that every tweet you send stands out to use Twitter cards. To ensure that the tweets include the image when people share your posts, make sure your website is set up with it. You can visit http://smo.knowem.com/ when your site has Twitter cards set up on it. On the Twitter tab, hit the click when you type in the address of your website, and if the setup of your Twitter cards is right, you will know by doing that.

Twitter followers building

Your brand will have increased benefits if your followers on Twitter are well-targeted and engaged. By using analytics and data to identify suitable conversations and users, you can increase your relevant Twitter followers with the use of a tool like Social Quant. Not only can you get more clicks and engagements into your site as your followers increase, but you can also select keywords to target.

Engage with influencers after identifying them

Your brand will gain to get more traffic to your website, more engagement, and also additional followers when you engage with influencers. With an influencer in your niche, you already have your audience. As a result, it's a huge advantage when you build great relationships with them.

To manage your contacts, use Twitter lists

Your timeline might feel overwhelming as you follow higher numbers of people. Instead of your main timeline, you can add people to your Twitter list to follow if you want to track tweets that are important or you want to track those people. Also, you use public lists created by other users through subscription or make a list you create private or public.

Email list target using Twitter ads

You can target your email list with your ads since, to hear more from you, they have chosen that. To target them when you have something to promote, Twitter will match with registered users those email addresses.

Hashtags' best practice

You can have 21 percent higher engagement than when, than those with 3 or more, your tweets' hashtags are 1 or 2. You must know that it is a bad idea if, you the sake of attracting attention, your tweets have every hashtag squeezed into them. Limit your choice of the hashtag per tweet to 1 or 2. And you may want to get on it if you are not using hashtags. Not only are they great to get people's attention, but they are also suitable for visibility.

Pinterest

On Pinterest, do you have a professional or personal brand? On Pinterest, as they come in several unique ways, there are many opportunities to meet your audience and also have your reach expanded. If your brand is on Pinterest, there are best practices and special notes that can add values to your brand as a sensational abode to iterate and test even as it falls under the umbrella of social media marketing. For your Pinterest marketing, here are some tricks to help you:

- Add a link to your pin description

- Write keyword-rich boards and descriptions

- Use text to create and pin images

- Use proper size to design images

- Create "pin it for later" links

- For your blog or website, apply for a rich pin

- Schedule your pins

- For 5 times at least daily, pin consistently

Here are some more Pinterest marketing tips for you:

Spread out your pins and pin more often

Increase your pin to have more Pinterest engagement, and the best practice is to do it for about 10 times a day. Pinning more often needs a few things for consideration, and some of them are:

- Spreading your pins will give your audience a useful experience. To avoid bursts of content, over time, it is in a queued schedule at Pinterest that these pins can arrive, instead of people seeing 10 pins in a row about social media tips.

- You will make your posting entirely stress-free for your brand when you schedule ahead of time. You can identify excellent content to share after finding them on Pinterest and then, through a few days, give them space when you place it into a schedule. You will be able to share a consistent volume of Pinterest content.

Request for your blog or website rich pins

You can add more considerable information and details on pins themselves when you make use of this free feature of Pinterest called rich pins. They are more of an open graph on Facebook or Twitter cards. As a pinner, you will have a better pinning experience, and it will be beneficial for your audience that sees your pins. Your rich pins can be a place, movie, recipe, product, or article.

Create images with the right sizes

With a minimum width of 600 pixels, Pinterest image is 1:3.5 or 2:3 as the best aspect ratio. The relationship between the image's height and the width is aspect ratio. We can have a 2:3 aspect ratio, for example, as:

- 800 pixels wide by 1,200 pixels tall

- 900 pixels tall by 600 pixels wide

Then, we can have an aspect ratio of 1:3.5 as:

- 2,800 pixels tall by 400 pixels wide

- 2,100 pixels tall by 600 pixels wide

Write detailed, keyword-rich, and better descriptions

Your pins description can add tons of values when you include some of these critical points:

- Give your audience something to engage them. At somewhere useful, add a link and share the next step if there is an action you want them to take.

- Positive sentiment

- It is acceptable for it to be a couple of sentences long

- Keywords

- Helpful details

Also, here are some best practices with more details from Pinterest:

- No references to Pinterest functionality

- No CTAs that are sales-y, such as buy now

- No promotional information

- No hashtags

- Use correct punctuation and capitalization

LinkedIn

You may be thinking of what LinkedIn has in stock for your brand to accomplish its marketing goals? Well, across the world, LinkedIn can connect your brand with more than 450 million professionals, whether you want to establish strategic partnerships, build brand awareness, or generate leads. If you want to grow your brand and engage your audience, here are some tips to about doing it successfully on LinkedIn:

Create an effective LinkedIn Company Page

Like your LinkedIn business profile, have a similar approach when it comes to your LinkedIn Company Page. To learn more about your company, prospective customers must get ample opportunity to engage with relevant content and the people who work in your company through your Company Page on LinkedIn. Right now, create a Company Page for your brand on LinkedIn to get started with marketing if you haven't.

Define your goals and audience

An excellent place to start is to define your goal, as with any marketing initiative. Your brand's marketing goals of LinkedIn comprise of raising awareness and lead generation. As such, it becomes easier for you to define your audience when you know what you want to accomplish.

Optimize your Company Page for search

On LinkedIn, for every effective Company Page, an audience is one common thing. You will have the chance to build your audience on Linked with these tips.

- Optimize your Company Page for search.

- Add a "follow" butting to your website

- Promote your Company Page outside the company

- Share relevant content

- Link to your Company Page

- Insert keywords

Add followers to Company Page

Your updates will start appearing directly in the LinkedIn feed of people when they follow your Company Page. With each update you publish, you will have a higher reach potential when you have more followers on your Company Page. To add followers, here are some tips to follow:

- Add a "follow" button to your website

- Promote your Company Page outside the company

- Start with employees

Increase Company Page engagement by using rich media

It is naturally quite faster than text for the brains of humans to process. As a result, text-only content has six times less engagement than posts with images. Add SlideShare presentations, videos, and images to your presentation for your brand to cater to the visual craving content by your audience.

Publish engaging content on your Company Page

Compelling content that will engage your audience must be the goal of your brand. And you will know you are engaging your audience with comments, shares, and clicks. On LinkedIn, even though for the benefits of your products and services, it can be tempting to sell to your audience, but sales-y content has poor performance. On your Company Page, content with thought leadership is all you need to learn to publish. Three types of thought leadership include:

1. Product thought leadership

2. Organizational thought leadership

3. Industry thought leadership

YouTube

From brands, YouTube doesn't always get the same considerations as Facebook and Twitter, even when it has been around for longer than them, and despite being the leader in online video consumption. However, the case is not the same again and will continue to change by the year 2020. When you want to create YouTube content for your company channel, you must adhere to a few tricks. You will get to create stellar content when you use effective CTAs, incorporate several formats for, and keep a consistent tone. Alternatively, you can sour your YouTube potential if you mix audiences and let 'going viral' be your focus. For your YouTube marketing success, here are some essentials to focus:

Use CTAs and keywords

In your video tags and video description, always include keywords. You must know that YouTube gets its treatment from several people as a video search engine since YouTube is the top video-sharing platform in the world. Also, there is a boost in the capabilities of its search with the fact that Google owns it. For you to tag your video with standard keywords, there is an option when you are uploading it. On YouTube, when people search, they will find your video. Some of the examples of CTAs are:

- Follow [insert your brand name] on social media

- Visit our website at [insert company URL] to learn more

- Give us a call today at [insert company phone number]

- Subscribe for more cool videos from [insert company name]

Don't attempt to go viral always

Your marketing goal must not always go viral even though with viral videos, your brand can get healthy engagement and make headlines. As opposed to how many views you can get, give your focus on your consumer and your brand when you are making videos for your brand. It is better to use your creative content over time for raving audience building even when views tend to be quite essential.

Conclude on your channel style and tone

You need to decide on the style of your YouTube channel with your team ahead of your video content creation planning on YouTube. Your audience will enjoy the video-viewing experience as you build an air of professionalism when, throughout your content, your style and tone are maintained consistently. Some questions that require your specific answers include:

- Do we have any industrial or YouTube influencers or personalities to collaborate with, and if yes, are we having guests in our videos?

- Are you hiring a professional videographer or an agency, or who will be responsible for our video creation?

- Are we thinking of having comedy in our videos?

- Are we going to make traditional advertisements, Q&As, tutorials, or what types of video content we want to make?

- Will there be staff members or actors in our videos?

- Are we proposing to have professional and sleek or friendly and hip, or which tone are we planning to convey to our videos?

- What should our CTA/CTAs be?

- What are our target demographics, and who is our audience?

Don't combine corporate and consumer content

There could be a temptation to have a few of your videos done for a corporate marketer or potential consumers when you are creating YouTube content. However, your channel may look awkward and disjointed, causing channel dissonance. For example, by trying to view on of your videos, viewers may discover that a video wasn't made for them, and as a result, getting them frustrated.

Instagram

There must be a good reason for your brand, these days, not to be on Instagram. If you have stores, it's time to get an account if your brand wants to get recognition from the people or whether you sell any physical product. It is vital for business as one aspect of our daily routines now is Instagram. Essentially, your requirement has to be a noble one if you need an Instagram marketing strategy. As such, here are some valuable information to get the strategy of your Instagram marketing running:

Audience understanding

Irrespective of your marketing, this point is quite crucial. What is the point if target prospects get no appeal from your Instagram content even when you have excellent content? Apart from knowing who you'd want your audience to be, you must also identify who is your current followers. You must find out whether they can, in some way, aid your brand building or are prospective consumers because you are using Instagram for marketing. So, how do you go about doing audience research? You need Instagram Insights. You will have interesting insights, using this tool, about those interacting and following your account. Also, you will have more insights into:

- Saves: how many people have saved your posts

- Video views: how often people view your video content

- Following action: daily on Instagram, how often are your followers on the platform

- Clicks on the website: has your brand profile's link received how many clicks

- Impressions: how many times people view your content

Talk *with* your audience, against at them

Never post too many sales materials to your followers by utilizing marketing on social media as an excuse. Much as you can, make sure you engage with your followers. Doing this makes your brand feel more human and less corporate. Also, it will be easier for different people to discover your comments when users comment and share them most times. Do this to have several feeds appearance since content with higher engagement gets priority from the algorithm of Instagram. You can encourage interaction by:

- Sharing their images

- Hold contest

Use relevant hashtags

For users to find your content more quickly, you can categorize and organize video and image content with the use of hashtags. Hashtags are virtually mandatory on Instagram since they are so popular. You must use hashtags if you want people to find your content. Best practices of hashtags are:

- Don't spam: keep them relevant to the image

- Never go overboard with tags: it is as good as useless to add #instagood or #love.

- Don't use too many hashtags: more than random 25 hashtags, target five effective hashtags

Create beautiful visuals

Quite essential for social media marketing is the practice of posting great content. Your brand's audience will keep coming back for more while it engages them with your brand. However, everything starts and ends with images on Instagram. It is for the opportunity of sharing photos that the whole network was created. If you are selling products online, this analysis is especially true. And it is on the visual appearance that 93 percent of the decisions in the buying process is based, according to one study. Since it is vital to have good images, to have more appealing content on Instagram, follow these tips:

- Choose a theme

- Change the subject and style

- Use tools to help

Snapchat

People don't longer use Snapchat only for sending between friends. There have been some developments with this social media channel. On your brand, the influence this marketing platform can have is not something you can't afford to ignore. As your target market, if Generation Z is your focus, this channel is an absolute necessity. That is because, as an aspect of routines daily, 71 percent of Gen Z makes use of Snapchat. Also, daily approximately 11 times, 51 percent of them use Snapchat. The older generations and adults are beginning to get hit with Snapchat's marketing penetrations; even teens are connected with its popularity.

If between 12 and 34 of ages, is the current target market of your brand, Snapchat is a viable marketing channel. However, as there would be a continuous adaptation of older generations to this platform, keep an eye on these trends. Active users of Snapchat daily are around 187 million in Q4 of 2017. In the last year, and in terms of daily users, with the continuous expectation of these trends in marketing, the platform has seen more than an 18 percent growth rate.

For your brand, what does this mean?

It's good news. For your brand to engage with your customers, now a different practical channel for marketing is available for you. However, if you have no knowledge about relating Snapchat to your customer and you have never used it before, this may be confusing or intimidating. Right now, for your brand, Snapchat can be viable with these incredible ways:

- Mix it up

- Inform your followers about an important milestone

- Drive traffic to your website

- Promote upcoming events

- Post relevant content

- Reply to your followers

- Provide exclusive access

- Promote a new product

- Take over another account

- Offer promo codes and discounts

- Always have post to your story

- Promote your Snapchat account on other marketing channels

- Create a sponsored lens

- Allow your account to be taken over by social influencers

- Feature content that is user-generated

There is a growing popularity for Snapchat, and you need to create an account for your brand right away if your company doesn't have an account. But you need to keep your followers engaged once you get them when your account is active. Overall, your Snapchat marketing strategy makes your brand better is what you want to ensure. Also, you want to drive sales as well as creating brand awareness.

Blog

A blog is not optional these days. It is the core foundation of strategy on social media marketing as an effective direct response. Before you start selling, your brand needs to utilize useful content to engage the audience into revenue after turning to the market. Make sure your content sells your solution, agitate the problem, let a problem get attention, and build trust. When you commit to your content plan throughout the year and have a schedule to stick to, you will see that it is not difficult to create a content plan. So, how does this work?

Set goals

For things you want to sell, setting goals using an approach that is detailed and specific with an integrated content plan. You can produce content which supports a clear vision with which you begin for the desired outcome. Through the blog, you can get more leads for your business, share case studies to build trust, establish yourself as an authority in the marketplace, and provide value to your audience.

Build an operational blog

You need to start with the end in mind and look for a great outcome when you want to blog in a most effective way. In your media platform, a blog is an editorial. You are the owner of this media. And whether your audience is small or big, you can use it any way you like since you control it. As it might involve your target audience for a subject, you can appropriately express your opinions on a subject on your blog. For your brand to zero in on what your audience finds essential, content should focus on the pains and interests of your prospects.

Write posts on social media

For the month, make use of the source for your posts on social media when you have your content written. With a focus on the theme of your topic on Facebook, Twitter, LinkedIn, and other platforms, engage your social network in an ongoing conversation. This way, still having in mind your sales strategy, you will have all your content created. To walk your prospect toward the sale is the role of your articles and posts.

Automate publication

For you to make this plan work for your brand, consistent and on-time delivery is a crucial part of it. You can schedule in advance your content to make sure of this. You will undoubtedly dread the situation of not having content you can use for your social media or a blog. For you to have your entire content on LinkedIn pre-program, Facebook, and Twitter, use a service like HootSuite or TweetDeck. Also, before your process of application, schedule your emails and blog posts.

At least, for once or twice a week, a relevant posting is a must for you, new content for blogs. You must also learn to keep to a schedule if you typically post for your readers to know which day. Use your social media network to promote these posts, and when posting new content, alert your readers through email.

Conclusion

Thank you for making it through to the end of *Social Media Marketing 2020: The Ultimate Step-By-Step Guide to Achieve Success, Learn the Best Beginner's strategy to Generate Powerful Content and Influence Fans and Followers*. Our hope is it was informative and able to provide you with all of the tools you need to achieve your goals, whatever they may be.

Chances are, you want to make a change if you have made it to this point. You want a turning point in your brand's social media marketing where not only your social marketing campaigns get tons of engagement, but also turn your followers to raving fans to go on to do the selling for you.

Imagine how your brand would grow if you have all the social media marketing tactics in the world, especially all tips and tricks in this book about things to avoid in the process of your social media marketing strategies. You will certainly be able to develop a hardcore social media content strategy.

Imagine how your business would grow if you could evoke strong positive emotion with your social media content as well as the strategies to create social media content and sharing. Imagine the power your brand can weird among your peers in the same industry if you have explicit knowledge about how you can successfully define and maintain your brand voice. You will be able to market your brand as if you were selling an individual with the power to be authentic and consistent with the use of some practical examples discussed in this book.

You have read about tips your brand can use to find its social media marketing voice. There are examples of how your brand can translate its voice to tone. Also, you have had an unfair understanding of ways to grow your social media presence to amplify your product marketing strategy. Life is all about making conscious decisions every day to strengthen your brand and increase your social media followers.

Finally, if you found this book useful in any way, a review on Amazon is always appreciated!